Resist Psychic Death: 250 Anecdotes

David Bruce

Published by David Bruce, 2022.

RESIST PSYCHIC DEATH: 250 ANECDOTES

First edition. September 4, 2022.

ISBN: 979-8215365373

Written by David Bruce.

Table of Contents

Dedication

DEDICATED TO MY SISTER MARTHA

Martha wrote, "When I was working at Longaberger, I worked with a girl who had two children and was in the middle of a divorce. She was so worried about Christmas for her boys. I received a very nice Christmas bonus that year, and I went to my boss and started a donation fund for the girl. My boss told me later that she — my boss —delivered the money to the girl's mother and father and told them not to tell her who brought the money for her. Months later the girl told me that the boys had the best Christmas that year, and she told me someone had brought money to her mom and dad for her, and she went to town and bought the boys Christmas. She never did know who did that for her. She was so thankful. I believe that I was the only one who donated to her, which was just fine."

***

The doing of good deeds is important. As a free person, you can choose to live your life as a good person or as a bad person. To be a good person, do good deeds. To be a bad person, do bad deeds. If you do good deeds, you will become good. If you do bad deeds, you will become bad. To become the person you want to be, act as if you already are that kind of person. Each of us chooses what kind of person we will become. To become a good person, do the things a good person does. To become a bad person, do the things a bad person does. The opportunity to take action to become the kind of person you want to be is yours.

Cover Photograph for *Resist Psychic Death: 250 Anecdotes* was taken by David Bruce

This is a short, quick, and easy read.

Anecdotes are usually short humorous stories. Sometimes they are thought-provoking or informative, not amusing.

***

Educate Yourself

Read Like A Wolf Eats

Be Excellent to Each Other

Books Then, Books Now, Books Forever

***

Do you know a language other than English? If you do, I give you permission to translate this book, copyright your translation, publish or self-publish it, and keep all the royalties for yourself. (Do give me credit, of course, for the original book.)

Chapter 1: From Activism and Activists to Comedians

Activism and Activists

• In Bikini Kill's early songs, vocalist Kathleen Hanna tends to repeat lines many times. She had a reason for doing this. The sound equipment Bikini Kill played live with was sometimes bad, and she worried that no one would understand the words, and so she repeated them over and over so that the audience would hear them. Some of the lyrics deserve to be heard over and over — for example, she repeated these lines from the song "Resist Psychic Death" over and over: "I resist with every inch and every breath / I resist this psychic death." Here's an example: Near the end of his life, the heart of Mexican artist José Clemente Orozco grew weaker, and his cardiologist, Dr. Ignacio Chávez, recommended that he stop the strenuous work of painting huge murals and instead concentrate on the less strenuous work of creating easel paintings. However, Mr. Orozco refused to take this advice. Instead, he remarked to his wife, "I'm not going to do as the doctor says and abandon mural painting. I prefer physical death to the moral death that would be the equivalent of giving up mural painting." So how does one resist psychic death? Some ways include practicing an art, appreciating various kinds of art, doing good deeds, paying attention to your soul as well as your body, staying angry at the things that should anger us, and being aware of the fabulous realities that surround us despite the presence of evil in the world.[1]

• In 2007, while standing in line in Victoria station in London, a man named Gareth Edwards, who describes himself as a "big, stocky bloke with a shaven head," noticed a well-dressed businessman cutting in line *behind* him. (Apparently, Mr. Edwards is so big that the businessman did not want to cut in line *ahead* of him.) Some people politely remonstrated with the businessman, but the businessman ignored the protests. So Mr. Edwards asked the elderly woman who was behind the businessman line-cutter-in, "Do you want to go in front of me?" She did, and Mr. Edwards then asked the new person standing behind the businessman line-cutter-in, "Do you want to go in front of me?" Mr. Edwards did this 60 or 70 times, so he and the businessman kept moving further back in line. Finally, just as the bus pulled up, the elderly woman whom he had first allowed to go ahead in line, yelled back to him, "Young man! Do you want to go in front of me?"[2]

• In November of 2010, tens of thousands of students protested in England over cuts in funding for education and higher fees for tuition that could keep them from getting a university education. Some students in London even attacked a police van, but a group of schoolgirls stopped the attack by surrounding the van and linking hands. *Guardian* journalist Jonathan Jones wrote, "Some who were at the student protests this week accuse police of deliberately leaving a solitary van in the middle of the 'kettled' crowd to invite trouble and provide incriminating media images of an out-of-control mob attacking it." (According to <en.wiktionary.org/wiki/kettling>, kettling is "The practice of police surrounding a hostile mob (usually of protesters) and not letting them disperse.") By stopping the violent students from attacking the police van, the schoolgirls helped prevent negative publicity about the student protests.[3]

• In 1977, future punk critic Steven Wells and some other punks wanted to go to a Mekons concert. However, the student rugby player who was at the door did not like the way that the punks were dressed and so refused to let them inside. The punks formed a picket line and informed everyone who came by what had happened and asked them not to cross the picket line. No one did. Twenty minutes went by, and the person who had organized the show came outside to find out why no one was going inside. The punks explained to him what had happened. The organizer then fired the rugby player and the punks enjoyed a good concert. (Rugby in England is class conscious. In the

South, Rugby Union is played by the posh. In the North, Rugby League is played by the working class. The Mekons concert happened in the South.)[4]

• In 1969 at Akron University, activist, artist, and musician Paul Mavrides and some of his activist friends announced that they were going to use their own homemade napalm to burn a puppy to death. Of course, this was a protest against the use of napalm to kill human beings in the Vietnam War. They planned to announce to the crowd that they had no napalm and no puppy, and then they planned to say, "How can you people justify showing up to save a *dog*, when there's an actual war going on and this napalm is being used on real people?" Unfortunately, the crowd that showed up was so angry that Mr. Mavrides and his activist friends had to be rescued by Akron University police, who smuggled them through underground tunnels to get them safely away from the angry crowd. And the use of napalm in Vietnam continued.[5]

• Alexander Campbell (1788-1866) was forced to take an examination in order to be admitted to the Lord's Supper at the University of Glasgow because the Lord's Supper was restricted to those deemed worthy to take it. After passing muster, participants were given a metallic token to present so they could partake of the Lord's Supper. Mr. Campbell, however, felt that the Lord's Supper should be open to all. Following his conscience, he declined to join the other participants, and he cast his metallic token into the plate as it was being passed round. The metallic token made a sound that echoed throughout the church.[6]

• Birth-control advocate Margaret Sanger looked shy and quiet, but she was tough and determined. Someone once asked her to take some time off for rest and relaxation, but she replied, "I am the protagonist of women who have nothing to laugh about." In 1916, she spent 30 days in jail after her birth-control clinic was shut down and she was charged with "illegal activity." After the 30 days were up, the police wanted to fingerprint her, but she did not want to be fingerprinted.

The result: She emerged from jail exhausted and bruised — and triumphant.[7]

• Saul Alinsky, an activist in Chicago, was upset when Station WGN decided not to show a film about Martin Luther because it was opposed by the archdiocese of Chicago. Mr. Alinsky tried to persuade Edward Burke, a monsignor of the archdiocese, to withdraw opposition to the film. Mr. Burke remained opposed to the showing of the film, so Mr. Alinsky said that it ought to be shown "with one proviso, that they show it backward so that Martin Luther will end up as a Catholic."[8]

• A notable act of activism occurred in Berlin when some activists painted some barrels to look like nuclear waste containers, filled them with sand, and then drove into Berlin and dropped them off in a place where they would be noticed. The news was filled with descriptions of the dangers of exposure to nuclear waste, and workers in Hazmat suits worked to remove the barrels. The activism created awareness of the risks of moving nuclear waste through populated areas.[9]

Advice

• Professor Ernst Schneidler taught many artists and illustrators, including Eric Carle, who created such books as *The Very Hungry Caterpillar* for children. Professor Schneidler was able to motivate his students to do their very best work, perhaps because he was so gifted at doing those things he taught. Actually, he did not spend a lot of time with the students; instead, he simply looked over their work every so often and pronounced judgment on it. Usually, he merely said "Dumb" or "Not dumb." When he said, "Good," which he rarely did, it was exceptionally high praise. He also spoke to the students on occasion. Professor Schneidler was gifted at determining what his students should do and what they should avoid doing: He knew his students' talents. When Mr. Carle tried to do calligraphy, Professor Schneidler told him, "Herr Carle, not so good. Dumb. Don't do that anymore. Anyway, we don't need any more calligraphers." But when Mr. Carle created some linoleum cuts, Professor Schneidler told him, "Good." However, Professor Schneidler added, "That's good, all right. But, ah! You don't even understand why it's good." This Mr. Carle interpreted as meaning, "Go and find out why it's good," which Mr. Carle considered very good advice.[10]

• *Sassy*, a magazine for North American teenage girls, once had a column titled "Dear Boy," in which girls could write a question about relationships and a famous guy would answer it. One girl wrote, "There's this guy I really like. He tells everyone that he doesn't even like me as a friend, but when we're alone together we do things that are reserved for people who think of each other as more than friends. What do I do?" The famous guy answering that question was Thurston Moore, vocalist and guitarist of the band Sonic Youth. He wrote, "The guy's a jerk. I know that won't discourage you from liking him, but he's got a major personality flaw: disrespecting you. Next time you're alone with him and he wants to get 'friendly,' tell him your friend Thurston Moore wants to kick his ass. And then tell him why."[11]

Animals

• A dog once saved the life of a Jew during the Holocaust. Ester Milshtein (a pseudonym) was first forced into the Warsaw Ghetto and then the Majdanek death camp near Lublin. Later, when she was 18 years old, she was transferred to the slave labor camp at Skarzynsko-Kamienna, where she made friends with the Kommandant's dog, a Great Dane she called Kelev. She talked to him, petted him, and sometimes she even ate some of his dog food, which was better than the food she and the other prisoners ate. Unfortunately, she contracted typhoid, which made her lose her hair and which reduced her weight to fewer than 80 pounds. At this time, she was 19 years old. Frequently, the prisoners were made to go through a selection process in which they were divided into two groups: One group would live, and the other group would die. Previously, she had survived several such selection processes, but this time, because of the effects of the typhoid, she was put in the group of people who would be murdered. While she was in this group of people, the dog she had named Kelev came to her, and she petted him and talked to him. The Kommandant noticed what she was doing, and he ordered her to be moved to the group of people who would live. Not long afterward, she was sent to work in a munitions factory in Buchenwald, and nine months later the Red (Russian) Army liberated her.[12]

• Eric Carle, author and illustrator of many children's books, remembers when some apples fermented in a wood, producing apples with alcohol. Two brown bears smelled the apples, and they enjoyed a feast — a feast that made them tipsy. Being tipsy, they did what bears — and lots of human beings — do. They took a nap to sleep it off. Soon, the human beings in the area learned about the tipsy bears, and a hunter realized that it would be easy (but of course not sporting) to kill the two sleeping bears. However, someone had telephoned the police, who sent two police officers in a patrol car to keep an eye on the bears. The hunter arrived first and left his truck, carrying a gun to shoot the bears. Immediately after the hunter had gotten out of his truck, the police officers arrived. The hunter jumped back in his truck and drove off. The police officers kept an eye on the bears until they woke up, shook themselves, and safely wandered away.[13]

• Following World War I was a period of unrest in Italy. During the unrest, 600 peasants, angry because they were out of work and hungry, broke down the gates of Enrico Caruso's villa and entered. When Mr. Caruso asked for a search warrant signed by the mayor, the peasants responded, "We are the mayor." He then asked that one car and enough food for 10 days be left behind, as after that time he and his wife would sail to America. The peasants wanted to take all the poultry, but Mr. Caruso asked that a white peahen be left alone, since she was sitting on 12 eggs due to hatch that day. The peasants laughed, said, "The signora is a peasant like us," and left the peahen alone. They also left behind a car and food. A few days afterward, the peasants sent to Mr. Caruso a small amount of money and a note expressing regret and gratitude.[14]

• Poet and essayist Tess Gallagher once had a horse that was named Angel Foot by her Uncle Porter, who wrote her, "Your filly is born. I have named her Angel Foot for the white on her hind foot where God must have held onto her when he dipped her into the black." Angel Foot played tricks on her owner. For example, she would gallop toward a barbed-wire fence, pretending not to see it, and then would stop suddenly with her nose close to the wire. One of Ms. Gallagher's friends asked her for a photograph of her sitting on the back of Angel Foot. He was waiting for a lung transplant, which he never got but which could have saved his life. Ms. Gallagher thinks that as he was waiting for the lung transplant, he needed "spirit-signs." She believes that such spirit-signs are comforting.[15]

Art

• The German artist George Grosz influenced a number of American artists, including Jack Levine. The American Institute of Arts and Letters once debated about whether to give Mr. Grosz or another artist an award. Member after member of the institute gave the opinion that Mr. Grosz had been great in his youth, but that in his later life he was not what he had been. Mr. Levine rose and spoke to defend Mr. Grosz: "Who of us, with the exception of maybe Jonathan Swift, is what he was?"[16]

• According to an old tradition, no one touches the person of the Pope. While painting a portrait of Pope John XXIII, American artist Bernard Godwin frequently rearranged the Pope's clothing, making the Pope's secretary and valet gasp, but the Holy Father simply smiled.[17]

Auditions

• When Patricia Birch was a soloist for the Martha Graham Dance Company, she auditioned for the part of Anybody in Jerome Robbins' *West Side Story*. When Mr. Robbins asked her if she could dance, she replied, "A little," so he left her with an assistant who would teach her the part so she could audition for it. By the next morning, however, Mr. Robbins had learned that she really was a dancer, so he told her, "I'm don't know what you're trying to pull here, but I'm on to you. Give me a triple knee turn!" The audition that followed was grueling, but she got the part.[18]

• When Merrill Ashley auditioned for the School of American Ballet, the whole thing took about 10 minutes, with dance teacher Antonina Tumkovsky twisting Merrill's legs around to see how flexible she was presently and how flexible she might become. She did pass the audition, was accepted into the SAB, and later found out that the report on her audition said, "Good feet, rather nice" — which was high praise for an audition at this particular school.[19]

Authors

• Lincoln Child, an editor at St. Martin's Press, invited Douglas Preston, a writer of columns about the American Museum of Natural History in New York, to write a history of the museum. Mr. Preston agreed, and the result is his book *Dinosaurs in the Attic*. Mr. Child wanted to have a *real* behind-the–scenes tour of the museum. Mr. Preston agreed, reluctantly, because Mr. Child did not have the security clearances needed to visit much of the museum. However, Mr. Preston decided to give him a tour at midnight because, he thought, no one would be around to check whether Mr. Child had the necessary security clearances. However, a museum guard appeared and boomed, "Who's there?" Mr. Preston thought that he was on the verge of being fired, but Mr. Child's quick wits came to the rescue. He told the security guard, "Thank God, you've finally found us! We've been wandering around for *hours* looking for the exit! How in the world do you get out of this place?" The adventure had a good result. While in the museum, with lightning flashes from outside the skylight making visible the dinosaur bones inside, Mr. Child said to Mr. Preston, "This is the scariest building in the world. Doug, we have to write a thriller set in a museum like this." They did. The thriller was titled *Relic*, and it introduced the character Aloysius X.L. Pendergast, who stars in a series of mysteries.[20]

• Judy Blume has written a number of books about the lovable boy called Fudge, who is based on her son Larry when he was young. Judy and a grown-up Larry once ate dinner with a little boy whose father read to him from the Fudge books each night. The little boy's father said to the little boy, "Do you know who this is? This is Judy Blume, who writes the Fudge books." The little boy's jaw dropped. Judy then said about Larry, "And guess who this is?" Larry said, "I was Fudge." The little boy's jaw dropped further.[21]

• World-famous make-up artist Kevyn Aucoin wrote three books. In his book *Making Faces*, he used his mother, Thelma, and his sisters, Carla and Kim, as models. After the book was published, people approached Thelma, Carla, and Kim and asked them for autographs. The book became a bestseller, and Kevyn was amused: "I'm a high school dropout with a *New York Times* bestseller, so the irony of that is hilarious.[22]

Children

• In January 2011, Cynthia Mello's water broke in Hartford, Connecticut. The weather was very bad and very snowy, but she needed to get to the hospital to give birth. She said, "I didn't think we were going to make it to the hospital on time. I told my husband to start shoveling the driveway. He came back in minutes later and told me there was too much snow." Her husband called 911, but of course the snow was a problem for the ambulance as well as for regular automobiles. What to do? Some people are problem-solvers, and this problem was solved. The ambulance made it to their home, and so did a snowplow. Mrs. Mello said, "The ambulance driver told me he had such a hard time getting to us. We live up on a hill, and they had a plow with them leading the way. The driver led us all the way to the hospital." They made it to the hospital, but the trip took two hours instead of the usual 20 minutes. Mrs. Mello said, "We were on I-84, and there were four tractor-trailers that had jackknifed. We had to turn around and take back roads to the hospital." Without the snowplow, they never would have made it. Pat McDonald, a nurse, said, "She called the ambulance because her water broke, and the next thing we know we have a snowplow leading her in the ambulance so she can have her baby on time." Baby Jack was born in the hospital, and he was immediately given a nickname: Jack Frost. (In a comment on this story, Bedford Brown wrote about a similar incident. At 2:30 a.m. on 27 January 2011, her son, Danny Brown, who lives in Danbury, Connecticut, called 911 because his wife, Stacey, was having labor pains. Mr. and Mrs. Brown received lots of help. An ambulance arrived, along with the Danbury Fire and Police departments, and *four* city snowplows to clear the way to the hospital, where a baby girl, Cameron Noelle Brown, was born at 5:42 a.m. Mother, daughter, and father are all doing well.)[23]

• As a famous comedian who performed in nightclubs, Danny Thomas traveled a lot. Often, his family would visit him for long weekends, staying in suites provided by the nightclub — Danny was a headliner. During one weekend visit, Danny was eager to be with his wife, but Tony, their son, developed a cold, and his wife insisted on sleeping in one of the twin beds in Tony's bedroom so that she could keep an eye on him. This went on for a couple of nights, with Danny becoming more and more frustrated. The morning of the third day, Tony was playing with a bucket of sand and a shovel, and he suddenly threw the bucket off the terrace, and the bucket dropped 12 stories to the ground. This frightened Danny, who told Tony, "Bad boy! Don't you know you could have hurt somebody by throwing that bucket off the terrace? Now go to your room and be quiet until I tell you to come out!" Tony started for his room, and then he turned around and said to his father, "Just for that, tonight she sleeps with me." Danny laughed and gave Tony a kiss. Tony's sister Marlo says about her brother, "Four years old and the kid's timing was impeccable."[24]

• Many young children are afraid of the barber, as Orlandor Davidson knows. Once, an 18-month-old boy actually did a somersault off the booster seat in the barber chair. Mr. Iverson froze, and the boy's father froze. Fortunately, another barber caught the boy before he hit the ground. By the way, Kwame Bandele remembers his first trip to the barbershop, although it was his babysitter who got the haircut. He was five or six years old, and he sat by the five- or six-year-old son of the barber. The barber was in a ranting mood, and he was saying things like, "What's got into these young kids? Runnin' around, lookin' like fools? Can't get no respect that way. Know what they need? They need a haircut and a shave. Now *that's* how you get respect." Young Kwame turned to the barber's young son and asked, "Does he want us to get a haircut and a shave?"[25]

• Joan and Nancy, the nieces of Alexander Woollcott, had vivid imaginations when they were young, and they created imaginary friends. Joan created a girl whose name was Alice, a French cow, a two-headed man, and some gnomes, Nancy created three fairies whose names were Rosabel, Gossamer, and Violetta. One day, Joan was angry at Nancy, and so she complained to their mother about Nancy's belief in Rosabel, Gossamer, and Violetta. Their mother, however, said, "Why shouldn't she have her fairies? You have Alice and the French cow, don't you?" Joan complained, "But don't you understand, Mother? My people are *real*!"[26]

• When Panio Gianopoulos, Molly Ringwald's husband, was four years old, his mother allowed him to walk to preschool all by himself — something that made him feel both proud and grown up. When he was grown up and a father who worried about the safety of his children (and who took his daughter to preschool), he asked his mother, "Are you completely crazy? You let me walk to school by myself! I was four years old!" His mother replied, "Of course I didn't let you. I kept about 20 feet behind you — close enough to make sure you were safe, but far enough so that you didn't know I was there and would feel like a big kid."[27]

• Art Linkletter knew about many, many funny happenings in families. For example, one small girl spent a lot of time watching workmen as they repaired the road in front of her house. Her grandmother, who was babysitting her, worried that she might annoy the workmen, so she said, "You shouldn't be out there bothering those workmen, dear." The small girl replied, "Oh, that's all right, Grandma. I'm intimate with only one of them."[28]

• Life is made of little moments that are often remarkable. In Rome, New York artist Raphael Soyer was sketching his wife and a wall of the Coliseum. A young boy of about eight sat by Raphael's wife, Rebecca. Raphael used sign language to ask him to remain there for a few moments, and then he put him in the drawing. When the drawing was done, he showed it to the boy, who looked at it and said, "*Bravo*."[29]

• Jeff Bezos, the founder of Amazon, has always loved numbers, even when he was a child. During a car ride with his grandmother, who was a heavy smoker, he calculated how many years her tobacco addiction would reduce her life expectancy. He thought that she would praise him for his mathematical ability; instead, she started crying.[30]

• Margret and H.A. Rey wrote and illustrated the Curious George books, which are about a curious monkey named George. Once, a small boy met the Reys. Margret remembers that the boy had "disappointment written all over his face" as he said, "I thought you were monkeys, too."[31]

• When renowned conductor Lorin Maazel was only seven years old, his mother discovered him with the score of Haydn's *Surprise Symphony* in his hands. She asked what he was doing with it, and he replied, "Reading it from top to bottom."[32]

• Elizabeth Gurney Dimsdale, a Quaker, once saw some small boys trying to ring a doorbell. She kindly rang the doorbell for them, but immediately the small boys ran away. She hesitated, and then she ran away, too.[33]

Christmas

• A few Christmas stories: 1) Brian Hyland's father liked some company at his home in Brick, New Jersey, during the holidays, but not too much and not too long. Therefore, to get rid of company when he got tired of it, he recorded a severe-winter-weather advisory on the Weather Channel and kept it for Christmas. When he felt that it was time for his company to go home, he played the tape and advised everyone to leave right away so that they would be safe at home before the winter storm struck. Brian says, "People grabbed their coats and high-tailed it out of there." 2) When Hailey Thompson of Westlake Village, California, was little, her father used to run around the house outside ringing sleigh bells loudly on Christmas Eve while her mother told her and her brothers that Santa Claus was flying over their house to deliver presents to the children in the neighborhood. 3) The father of Jonathan Alpert, who is the author of the syndicated column *No More Drama*, used to disguise his voice by putting wax paper in his mouth and then telephone kids in the neighborhood to say, "Ho ho ho! This is Santa Claus. Have you been a good boy this year? What would you like for Christmas? Don't forget to leave me cookies and milk." One year the wax paper did not disguise his voice well enough, so a neighborhood boy said to him, "Mr. Alpert, I know this is you. The real Santa called an hour ago."[34]

• A nurse once told K. Lynn Wieck, who is also a nurse, about working with leukemia patients at a time when nearly all of them died (things are different now) and when hospitals did not allow children to visit (things are different now). She was caring for a 32-year-old man whom she knew would soon die. It was the Christmas season, and she says, "I asked him what he wanted for Christmas that day and he told me that all he wanted was to see his children. I made a decision I have never regretted." The nurse talked to the man's wife and had her bring the children to the hospital the next day, when the nurse, after her strict supervisor had left, allowed the wife and children to visit the seriously ill man. The nurse saw the young children, who were happy to be with their father, who had a wide smile on his face. The family was able to truly visit and create good memories. The day after the visit, with his wife by his side, the father died.[35]

• Reporter Omar Villafranca is correct when he writes, "Santa speaks all languages — even the ones that can't be heard." For example, in December of 2010 Santa spoke in American Sign Language to over 150 children who came to see him at the Shops at Willow Bend in Plano, Texas. Mesquite Lawrence Elementary schoolteacher Sarah Schubert said, "This is truly the best thing that happens to our kids all year long. They came up to me this morning and said, 'You know that Santa can sign with us?' I mean, they get that!" Santa told Mr. Villafranca, "I sign to them and say, 'Come up and see Santa Claus,' and their eyes and their mouths are just open wide and they go, 'Wow!' And sometimes they just run and their expression is just, it's — it's priceless." Weston Teel, who is eight years old, asked Santa for a bubblegum machine and a popcorn machine.[36]

• At a Christmas pageant, young Paul Candler Porter had to play a barefooted shepherd. He wasn't interested in being in the pageant, but being the son of a preacher, he knew he couldn't get out of it. Still, he wished to find a way to make it more interesting. During the pageant, young Paul stood still and looked down at his feet, and all of the other children in the pageant kept breaking out in laughter, although they tried to stifle it. After the pageant was over, Paul's parents found out what had happened. Young Paul had drawn funny faces on his feet and during the pageant had amused himself — and the other children in the pageant — by moving the muscles in his feet to make the faces change expression.[37]

• In a Nativity play acted by 1st-graders, Mary was attended by a physician, who announced to Joseph after the birth of Jesus, "Congratulations — it's a God."[38]

Church

• During church service, Barbara McKeever's grandson told her that a woman singing a solo couldn't sing very well. She answered, "She sings from her heart, so it's good." Afterward, she was singing along with the car radio, and her grandson told her, "You sing from the heart, too, don't you?"[39]

• Church of Christ preacher Raccoon John Smith spoke about Repentance for several Sundays in a row. When his congregation complained, Raccoon John replied, "When you *do* it, I'll quit preaching on that and take up something else."[40]

Clothing

• In July 2008, Mary J. Blige overheard a stranger at the Diane von Furstenberg store in New York talking to a sales assistant about a dress. The customer had a $900 dress on hold, but she was dismayed when she heard the price because she had thought the dress cost $500, and she couldn't afford $900. Ms. Blige gave the woman $400. At first, the woman did not want to take the money, but Ms. Blige said, "I know what it's like to want something and not be able to have it. I insist." The woman then accepted the money, but said that she wanted to send Ms. Blige a check when she had the money. Ms. Blige declined the offer, saying, "Just enjoy it. I'm blessed, so let me do this."[41]

• Opera singer Mary Garden led a fairly simple life. Once, she and her sister Aggie were traveling out west on a train. Aggie wore a very nice nightgown made of silk and lace, while Mary had cold cream on her face, and was wearing a shawl and knitted cap to keep her warm. Aggie looked at her and said, "Mary, what an awful-looking woman you are! Shall I tell you something? If this train is wrecked tonight and both of us are killed, I shall probably be buried as the beautiful Mary

Garden." Mary asked, "And I?" Aggie replied, "You will be buried as Mary Garden's maid."[42]

• English fans of punk rockers sometimes engaged in gobbing — spitting on punk rockers as they performed. Supposedly this was a compliment, although as you would expect often the punk rockers did not like it. English singer Honey Bane once performed a concert wearing a raincoat and holding an umbrella. After her performance, the raincoat and umbrella were drenched with saliva, but she was dry.[43]

• Rabbi Joshua ben Levi visited Rome, where he saw a homeless man wearing rags on a street lined with statues adorned with expensive clothing. He prayed, "O Lord, here are statues of stone covered with expensive garments. Here is a man, created in Thine own image, covered with rags. A civilization that pays more attention to statues than to living men shall surely perish."[44]

• Choreographer John Taras wore good clothing — Pierre Cardin created many of his outfits. Mr. Taras also wore what he considered a good fragrance — Vetiver — although some other people disagreed about that. One day, Mr. Taras got in a taxi, and the driver sniffed and then asked him, "Hey, mister, do you smell something burning back there?"[45]

Comedians

• Cheech and Chong do stoner comedy, and their fans really get into it. For example, as Cheech and Chong were performing in Eugene, Oregon, a fan threw a gift for the duo onto the stage. Mr. Chong said, "I thought it was just a joke at first when somebody threw a 3-foot joint onstage. But it was full of bud, the most I've ever seen in one joint. A guy could go to jail for a long time with that much in his house." Once in a while, they forget a line from a classic routine. No problem — their fans yell out the line to them. And sometimes they meet a fan who tells them about reciting one of the duo's classic routines in the fan's 3rd-grade classroom — and getting suspended from school.[46]

• In the early 1980s, insult comedian Judy Tenuta and comedian Tommy Hack worked together. They were going to do a gig in the badlands of South Dakota. Mr. Hack was driving — it was his Ford Pinto — and about 100 miles from their destination he asked Ms. Tenuta, "Hey, Judy, you saw my act last night, so what do you think of it? Be honest, what do you really think?" She replied, "Ask me when we get within walking distance of the town."[47]

• Occasionally, we hear of celebrities demanding odd things in their dressing rooms. Sometimes, the celebrity has a good reason for odd requests. For example, comedian Totie Fields demanded in her contract that 12 cups of coffee be brought to her dressing room. Why? Because as a struggling young comedian, she had been unable to have even one cup of coffee brought to her dressing room.[48]

Chapter 2: From Conductors to Food

Conductors

• Lieder singer Lotte Lehmann was frightened of Arturo Toscanini because of his reputation, and she found working with him a "fearful pleasure." Still, shortly after singing for him for the first time, she was relieved to sing a few lieder for a Beethoven association. Before performing, she told a friend, "Oh, I feel so calm. An easy program, a nice appreciative audience, and no Toscanini there to be frightened of." At that moment, she looked out at the audience — and saw Toscanini.[49]

• Georges Enesco, a Romanian conductor, was beloved of orchestras. For one thing, he did not pretend to know everything. While guest-conducting the New York Philharmonic, he declined to have intensive rehearsals of Johannes Brahms' Fourth Symphony, instead telling the musicians, "Gentlemen, you know the work better than I do." Of course, this made the musicians eager to perform well to prove themselves worthy of Maestro Enesco's praise.[50]

• Sir Thomas Beecham disliked the music of Vaughan Williams. At one rehearsal, he conducted a Williams symphony, but he seemed to be paying very little attention to it. In fact, after the symphony was over, Sir Thomas continued to move his baton until a member of the orchestra told him, "It's finished, Sir Thomas." Sir Thomas looked at his score and said, "So it is — thank God!"[51]

• All of the rehearsals of the Boston Symphony Orchestra under Maestro Serge Koussevitzky were intense. Even very popular and often-played pieces were approached anew each time they were to be played. According to Maestro Koussevitzky, whatever the orchestra was playing was "the greatest of the greatest" — otherwise, they would be playing something else.[52]

• Conductor Arturo Toscanini sometimes got very angry at his musicians. Often, he would break his baton in anger. Once, his baton would not break, so he took out his handkerchief and tried to tear it; however, it would not tear. Therefore, Mr. Toscanini took off his coat and tore it to shreds. Feeling much better, he continued the rehearsal.[53]

Couples

• Danielle Fishel, young actress in the TV series *Boy Meets World*, once had a jealous boyfriend while she was still in school. She had been going with her boyfriend for about three weeks, and when she was talking with a male friend named Matt whom she had not seen for a while, her boyfriend grabbed her arm and said, "What are you doing?" She explained that she was talking with a friend, and he told her, "You should not be over here talking, and all my friends want to know what my girlfriend is doing talking to another guy." Then he tried to pull her away. She told him, "Excuse me? You can tell your friends that if they have a problem, they're not part of our relationship. And if it's you who has the problem, you can turn around and say bye right now because I want to talk to Matt." That was the end of the relationship. And good riddance.[54]

• Comedian Bob Zany once talked with a woman in the audience and learned that she had recently gotten engaged. He asked her, "When did you know he was the one?" She replied, "When the stick turned blue."[55]

Crime

• Bruce Simms is a barber in Congress Heights, Washington, D.C. — a tough area. One night, he was robbed in his barbershop, along with everybody else. Two men wearing ski masks came in and ordered everyone on the floor. Mr. Simms had $1,500 cash money on him — $300 in one pocket for making change, and $1,200 in another pocket in case someone came along selling a stolen big-screen TV. He threw the $1,200 behind some boxes and dropped the $300 in front of him for the robbers to pick up. The robbers got his $300, his wallet, his watch, and his rings. Later, he found out that almost immediately after leaving the barbershop the robbers shot and killed a man. After they left, his telephone rang. He answered it, and his four-year-old daughter said, "Daddy, I love you." Mr. Simms started crying. He says, "I had almost left the shop ten minutes before those guys robbed us. If I had, I'd still have my stuff. But I would have missed out on a lesson: *things* can blind you, hold you back. This life is more than money or a watch or a few rings. I have a daughter ... and she loves me. How much is that worth?" After being robbed, Mr. Simms got a new business card. It shows him kneeling in church at the altar. When people ask what his new business card is about, he replies, "It's about gratitude."[56]

• Helena Rubinstein left Poland and traveled to Australia with 12 pots of facial cream that had been made by a Hungarian doctor. The Australian women liked the facial cream's effect on Helena's complexion, and Helena recognized a business opportunity. She became very, very rich through selling her cosmetics and through her determination — a trait that served her well throughout her life. When she was 94, some armed robbers broke into her apartment in Manhattan. She told them, "Go ahead and kill me — I am not going to let you rob me." The armed robbers ran away.[57]

• Rebbe Wolfe used to pray every night and revoke his right to all his possessions, saying to God that everything he owned no longer belonged to him. Why? So that if a thief should come in the night and carry away some of his "possessions," the thief would not have violated God's law: Thou shalt not steal.[58]

• Rabbi Levi Isaac of Berdychev was a good man who thought the best of others. Once, the good Rabbi heard a thief boasting to other thieves about how much he had stolen, and he said, "It is still a long time to Selichot, yet the man has already began to confess his sins."[59]

• Daigan, a Zen monk, was studying when a thief walked into his apartment and robbed him. As the thief was leaving, Daigan asked him to shut the door to keep the thieves out.[60]

Critics

• Sir Neville Cardus, a critic, once complained in print that Sir Thomas Beecham had conducted at a much too rapid tempo the final act of *Siegfried*, thus marring an otherwise fine performance. Sir Thomas, of course, had an explanation. He told Sir Neville that the orchestra had been in the pit since 5:30 p.m., the pubs closed at 11 p.m., the audience had homes to get to, and so, after looking at his watch just before the final act and discovering that it was already after 10 p.m., he had decided to conduct the final act quickly and let everyone go about their business.[61]

• Austrian Emperor Joseph II once said about Wolfgang Amadeus Mozart's *Die Entführung aus dem Serail*, "Too beautiful for our ears and a great many notes, my dear Mozart." Mozart replied, "Exactly as many as are necessary, Your Majesty."[62]

• German composer Max Reger did not take criticism lightly. He once wrote a critic who had savaged his work: "I am sitting in the smallest room in the house. I have your review in front of me. Soon it will be behind me."[63]

• Pianist Moriz Rosenthal disliked much modern music. He once listened to three piano students rehearsing three different pieces of music at a school for pianists, then said, "Ah, modern music."[64]

Death

• Sometimes people die of hunger; sometimes this happens because of pride. In Vilna in the 19th century, a rich man became poor. Because of his pride he kept up appearances, and he did not ask for help, and so he died because of lack of food. The townspeople were ashamed that anyone could die in their midst in this way, but Rabbi Israel Salanter (1810-1883) told them, "That man did not die of starvation, but of excessive pride. Had he been willing to ask others for help and admit to his situation, he would not have died of hunger."[65]

• Elimelekh of Lyzhansk (d. 1786), a Hasidic Rebbe, felt that when he died, he would be asked several questions in the Heavenly court of justice: Had he been as just as he could have? Had he been as charitable as he could have? Had he studied as much as he could have? Had he prayed as much as he could have? To each of these questions, he would have to answer, "No." However, he also believed that "the Supreme Judge will smile and say, 'Elimelekh, you spoke the truth. For this alone you will have a share in the world to come.'"[66]

• According to the Midrash, when you die, you will have three friends. Your first friend — money — will not go with you when you die. Your second friend — your family and neighbors — will go with you only as far as your grave. Your third friend — your good deeds — is the only friend who will accompany you to the next World and defend you before the Judge.[67]

• Tenor Enrico Tamberlik was able to read his own highly complimentary obituary notices after a rumor started in 1882 that he had died. He pasted the notices in an album and enjoyed reading them until his death seven years later.[68]

• When Mulla Nasrudin realized that he was dying, he decided to play one final joke. He ordered that his tomb have a huge, locked door to keep intruders out, but he also ordered that his tomb not have any walls.[69]

Education

• African-American bandleader Cab Calloway was a leader, and he taught his musicians a lot. One thing that he taught them is the importance of punctuality. He would say, "I gotta be here — you better be here." He also fired a trombone player, Claude Jones, because of a lack of punctuality. In addition, he told his musicians, "Cleanliness is next to godliness." One of the subtexts to that saying was that he was a sharp-dressed man, and he expected the musicians in his band to be sharp-dressed men. He bought them the clothing they wore on stage, and they bought their own sharp clothing to wear on the street. If a band member had a hole in his undershirt, another band member would give him a friendly warning: "You better watch those holes, man, or the bat's gonna get you." If he kept wearing the undershirt with the hole, someone would put his finger in the hole and say, "Did you call me a son of a b*tch?" Then he would walk off with his finger still in the hole and tear the undershirt. Even if the victim got angry, he did not fight because all of the other members of the band were in favor of being sharp-dressed. If a band member's hat started to look greasy or ragged, someone would throw it in the trash. When the band member asked if anyone had seen his hat, someone would reply, "Maybe the bat got it." By the way, one of the things that even a sharp-dressed man has to do occasionally is to empty his bladder, and when you're on a tour bus without a bathroom and in a hurry to get to your destination, the bus can't always stop. So the members of the band worked out a system. The band member with the full bladder would go to the front of the bus and yell, "Oil change." That was the signal for everyone on that side of the bus to roll up his window. Then the bus door would open and the band member would empty his bladder from the moving bus.[70]

• Ross P. Mayo, a male nursing student working in the nursing station at an elementary school, ran into a problem when a little girl named Tammi came in to have a scratch treated. Even though he told her, "I am a nurse. I can help you. Trust me," Tammi was terrified because she thought that all nurses were female and she did not know who this strange man was. Fortunately, Ms. Walker, the school nurse, walked in and reassured Tammi. Even then, Tammi did not believe that Ross was a nurse. Ross asked Tammi why she did not believe that he was a nurse, and Tammi answered, "Because you're not a lady." Therefore, Ross decided to teach the students that some nurses are men. He addressed the 2nd-grade students because he felt that they would be able to understand what he had to say to them. He turned it into a game and had the children determine his occupation by asking him questions. It took a while, with the children guessing that he was a doctor or a dentist, but finally they figured out that he was a nurse. Ross was able to explain in words that the children could understand that some women are doctors and that some men are nurses. Before the meeting, the children had written about nurses. After the meeting, he had the children write again about nurses. The writing showed that the children had learned a lot about nurses. A sample BEFORE paper: "I think a nurse is a nice lady who helps people." A sample AFTER paper: "A nurse can be a lady or a man. Nurses are working in clinics, schools, and hospitals. And some nurses are going to people's houses, too. And a lady can be a doctor."[71]

• A controversy arose in the early 2010s about a mosque being erected near Ground Zero — that is, near the site of the former World Trade Center, which was destroyed in the infamous 11 September 2001, terrorist attack. Actually, the "mosque" would have been a community center with a prayer room rather than a mosque, but most people railing against the "mosque" did not know that. In the United States, of course, the First Amendment guarantees the freedom of religion, but many people railing against the "mosque" seem not to know that. Two women who did understand that, and who understood something that Roger Ebert wrote ("Where one religion can build a church, so can all religions") were a couple of strippers near the 9-11 site. Cassandra was a stripper at New York Dolls. At first, she was concerned that the call to the five daily prayers of Islam would annoy the neighbors, but once she learned that no loudspeakers would be used, she said, "I don't know what the big deal is. It's freedom of religion, you know?" And Chris, a stripper at the Pussycat Lounge (and a Red Cross volunteer who helped 9-11 survivors, and a woman who lost eight firefighter friends and neighbors on 9-11) said, "They're not building a mosque in the World Trade Center. It's all good. You have your synagogues and your churches. And you have a mosque."

Mr. Ebert wrote, "Cassandra and Chris reflect American values more instinctively and correctly on this issue, let it be said, than Sarah Palin, Howard Dean, Newt Gingrich, Harry Reid and Rudy Giuliani, who should know better."[72]

• At a family gathering that included nine-year-old Joan, the niece of drama critic Alexander Woollcott, the rich patriarch of the family looked around, smiled, and announced to all, "I will give $50,000 to the parents of my first great-grandchild." Excited by the offer, Joan asked, "Grandfather, does it have to be legitimate?" Joan was quite a character. She was the second oldest child, and she started school at the same time as her older sister because she did not want to be parted from her. They went through 1st grade together, but the school authorities decided to keep Joan back because of her age, although she had passed first grade. Joan did not agree with the decision. She went to the 2nd-grade classroom, and even after she was sent to the 1st-grade classroom, she kept showing up in the 2nd-grade classroom, sitting at an empty desk, and laying her 2nd-grade homework in front of her. One day she showed up at school with a bouquet of flowers. The 1st-grade teacher said to her, "Joan, dear, what perfectly lovely flowers!" Joan replied, "Thank you, but they are not for you." Joan then went to the 2nd-grade classroom and presented the flowers to the 2nd-grade teacher. After a few weeks, the school authorities gave up and let Joan stay in the 2nd grade.[73]

• Doug Butler teaches the craft of farriery (equine hoof care, including making horseshoes and fitting them to the hooves of the horse). When his son wanted to learn the craft, he told him, "Get a hundred pieces of steel and turn them into a toe bend and then bring them back to me." His son did that; it took him several days. Next Mr. Butler told his son, "On each of the ends, make a heel." He did that — for a total of 200 heels. What was the result of all that work? Mr. Butler says, "By the time he got to number 195, he could make a good heel." Mr. Butler's mentor was a Scottish master blacksmith named Edward

Martin. In Colorado, Mr. Martin judged a horseshoe-making contest in which Mr. Butler competed. When Mr. Martin arrived, he did not just judge the contest; he also made horseshoes. The competition organizers told him, "You don't have to make the shoes. You're the judge. We flew you over here from Scotland, and we don't expect you to make the horseshoes." Mr. Martin replied, "If you can't make the shoes, you've got no right to judge." Mr. Butler says, "So he made them, in a lot less time than it took us, and they were better than any that we made. So we had great respect for anything he would say to us. There was no murmuring about his judging."[74]

• In the late 1950s, Eileen Birin taught at a parochial school in Dallas, Texas. She had an unmotivated 7th-grade student named Scott, who received all F's on his report card. He even received a lecture from the monsignor because of his grades. The next day Scott went to school with his face a mess of black, purple, and blue bruises. He also wore a bloody bandage on his head. One of the students told Ms. Birin that Scott's father had beaten him because of all the F's on his report card. Ms. Birin felt awful, of course, but she began teaching and assigned the students some math problems to do in class. While working on the math problems, Scott rubbed his face, and part of a bruise disappeared from his face and appeared on his hand! Ms. Birin looked closely at the "bruises" and discovered that they were really made of make-up. She told Scott, "You'd better go to the washroom and get that gunk off your face." Scott washed his face, and over time his grades improved, and although Ms. Birin has not seen him for a while, when the credits roll after she sees a movie, she looks for his name among all the make-up artists.[75]

• A man went to a monastery and asked a monk a question about Buddhist teaching. Because the monk was silently meditating, he did not reply, so the man went away, angry. The next day, the man returned and asked a different monk the same question. The monk gave him a long answer, but the man was furious at the length of the answer and went away, still angry. Again, the next day the man returned and asked his question of a third monk, who was aware of what had happened the previous two days. This monk gave a medium-length answer, but the man accused him of treating the matter sketchily and again went away, still angry. The third monk explained the matter to the Buddha, who replied, "There is always blame in this world. If you say too much, some people will blame you. If you say a little bit, some people will blame you. If you say nothing at all, some people will blame you."[76]

• Amy Votava teaches children about accepting other people, including fat people. She tells them about an experiment in which children were shown drawings of a child of normal weight and of children with handicaps and of a fat child. Children said that the depiction of the fat child was a depiction of a person who was "lazy, dirty, stupid, ugly, cheats, and lies." Not all children, however, feel that way. After teaching one group of kids about body size, Ms. Votava told them about the experiment and then asked, "Now that you have had these lessons about body size, what would you do if you had to pick the least likable child?" One girl raised her hand and replied, "I would say, 'How can you expect me to do this when I have no idea who these people are on the inside?'" Ms. Votava remembers, "Thirty-nine other heads nodded in unison."[77]

• When Rabbi Joseph Telushkin was a student at Yeshiva University, a certain professor was blind, but was still able to teach because he had memorized so much of the Talmud. This professor had one small problem — he knew the name of only one student in the class, so he called on that student every day to read and explain the part of the Talmud being studied that day. This was driving the student crazy. One day, the professor, as usual, called on the student to read the text out loud, but the student spoke up, disguising his voice and saying that the student the professor had asked for wasn't present that day because of illness. "He's not here?" said the professor. "Then you read the Talmud out loud today."[78]

• When Molly Ringwald was in the 2nd grade, she wanted to be a jazz singer. (Today, she sings jazz in a group for fun.) When her class was given the assignment of doing a presentation on a great USAmerican hero, most kids did their projects on such prominent USAmericans as George Washington, but she did her project on the prominent USAmerican jazz singer Bessie Smith. On American Life Story day, she showed up at school dressed in 1920s clothing, and she performed a few Bessie Smith songs such as "Gimme a Pigfoot and a Bottle of Beer." (Molly says, "Miss Kestenbaum was a very progressive 2nd-grade teacher.")[79]

• When Sharon Salzberg and others established the Insight Meditation Society in Barre, Massachusetts, in 1975, she began a week of intense meditation. Unfortunately, it was a very boring week, and as she sat meditating on lovingkindness and directing lovingkindness toward herself, she felt as if she were accomplishing nothing. But when she was packing some belongings, she dropped a jar, which shattered. Her first thought was, "You are really a klutz, but I love you," and her second thought was, "Wow! Look at that. Something did happen in this week of practice."[80]

• Tenor Rolando Vallazón was discovered — in a way — in the shower. At age 11 or 12, he was singing a song by Baloo from *The Jungle Book* in the shower when the director of the Academy of Performing Arts heard him and knocked on the door. He asked Rolando's mother, "Who's singing up there?" She replied, "I'm sorry. I'll tell him to shut up." He objected, "No, no. We're starting a program for young people, and maybe he'd be interested in singing." Rolando went there, he discovered that he enjoyed being on stage, and now he has an international career singing in opera.[81]

• Very often, the Navajo do important actions just before dawn. When 10-year-old Jaclyn Roessel and her Nalí Ruth ("nalí" means "father's mother or father") went searching for wild plants to use to dye wool, they did so early in the morning. Jaclyn asked, "Why do we always do things when it is still dark?" Nalí Ruth answered, "The Holy People [Navajo spiritual beings] taught us that there is wisdom and beauty in the darkness before dawn. If you sleep in, you miss it." By the way, the Navajo have a wide meaning for the word "aunt." An aunt is any older female relative.[82]

• A man of wit, author George Plimpton once had a calling card that said, "If you plan to commit arson, murder, larceny, adultery, etc., notify George A. Plimpton, *Boston Herald* correspondent." And supposedly, when he left Cambridge, he had to take a three-hour test that had exactly one question: Who was Charles James Fox?" Mr. Plimpton had no idea who Charles James Fox was, so he made up stuff up: "Charles James Fox was a rather mediocre second baseman for the Cincinnati Reds ...."[83]

• In June of 2010, Jane Schwanbeck retired from Lomarena Elementary School in Laguna Hills in South Orange County, California, after 37 years as a kindergarten teacher — she spent 36 of those years in the same room! When she retired, her students gave her testimonials. For example, TJ, who was in her kindergarten class that year, said, "I feel like she's the best teacher I've ever had." And Kirsten said what many students said, "What I'm going to say is that I love my teacher."[84]

• Architect Frank Gehry designed the Ray and Maria Stata Center for Computer, Information, and Intelligence Sciences at the Massachusetts Institute of Technology. Mr. Gehry knew that MIT is noted for its "endless corridor" — a corridor that winds throughout the school, so he designed a Student Street for the Stata Center and connected it to the endless corridor. Apparently, students approved of it because one student wrote on a chalkboard, "Frank Gehry, we love you."[85]

• Lynn Frances Anderson started out playing guitar and mandolin, but when she was in the 5th grade, she hid her brother's trumpet in the family pet's doghouse one evening, and the next morning she smuggled it onto the bus so that she could learn to play it in the school band, although her mother had declined to sign her up for band. Fortunately, her mother was flexible. Ms. Anderson says, "She thought if I went to that much effort, she might as well let me learn."[86]

• A friend of Sharon Salzberg once attended a three-month meditation retreat at the Insight Meditation Center in Massachusetts. He had several difficult days at the retreat, and finally he decided to leave the retreat, check into a motel, and watch a football game on TV. He did, and when he returned to the retreat, he was overcome by guilt. He told his teacher, Dipa Ma, what he had done. She looked at him, held his hand, and said, "That's okay. Now you can start again."[87]

• Franz Liszt once read a score by a young man who could not write music. Liszt pointed to a place on the score, and then said, "This must not be done in music." The young man haughtily replied, "But I have done it." Liszt dipped his pen in an ink well, then splattered the ink all over the young man's white waistcoat, and said, "This, too, *can* be done, but it *must* not be." Then Liszt bought the young man a new white waistcoat.[88]

• Kato-Dewanokami-Yasuoki revered the martial arts. One day, Zen master Bankei visited him, and Yasuoki picked up his spear and pointed it at Bankei. However, Bankei merely used his rosary to flick the point of the spear aside, and then told Yasuoki, "No good. You're too worked up." Eventually, Yasuoki became a master of the spear and spoke of Bankei as having been his greatest teacher in that art.[89]

• The Hasidic master Israel of Rizhin used to teach by using parables. For example: A traveler is alone on a road, trying to reach a town where he will be safe. It is night, and there is a lightning storm. If the traveler is foolish, he will look at the lightning and become more afraid, but if the traveler is wise, he will look at the road, which is well lit by the lightning.[90]

• Hasidic Rabbi Meyer Premishlaner once pointed out that God gave us two eyes although we could see with only one eye. Why did

God give us the extra eye? According to the Rabbi, "The answer is this: One eye is for seeing our neighbors' virtues, and the other eye is for seeing our own failings."[91]

Fame

• Makeup artist Kevyn Aucoin once said, "Everyone has the potential to look beautiful." Don't believe it? Believe it! Many models for his second book about makeup, *FaceForward*, were, as you would expect, famous actresses and models; however, many were so-called "ordinary" women, including his mother, Thelma Aucoin, whom he made up and photographed as herself, a 66-year-old mother and grandmother. The book also features transformations such as Liza Minelli transformed into Marilyn Monroe — and his mother transformed into Marlene Dietrich. Mr. Aucoin even asked a total stranger, Louisa Lee, whom he met while shopping, to allow him to make her up so he could put her in his second book. He also asked the same thing of sales associates (Angela Barrett and Marleen Everett), a gal Friday (Maryliam Crespi), and a friend's mother (64-year-old Bobbie Reuter, who was born in Korea). By the way, Mr. Aucoin worried that whenever he would ask a total stranger to let him put her in a book, it would sound like a pickup line. However, since Mr. Aucoin was an out and rather flamboyant gay man, I'm not sure that many women thought that he was trying to pick them up.[92]

• The famous cellist Pablo Casals went to a physician who had attended President Eisenhower. Mr. Casals congratulated him, saying that the physician was a very famous man. The doctor humbly replied that he would never be as famous as Mr. Casals. Mr. Casals thought a moment, and then admitted, "That's true."[93]

• Lieder singer Lotte Lehmann's chauffeur, whose name was Fritz, was an unlikely celebrity; however, he was proud when a newspaper published a photograph of himself and an operatic notable. The caption of the photograph identified the people depicted as two "notabilities."[94]

Fans

• Jonathan Kellerman's first mystery, *When the Bough Breaks*, appeared in 1985 and introduced the character Alex Delaware, who thereafter starred in many of his mysteries. The book was not supposed to be a hit, but it got rave reviews and became a word-of-mouth — and definitely a surprise — bestseller. That is why Mr. Kellerman answers fan mail. He says, "But for the graciousness of ordinary folk who took the time to traipse to the bookstore and plunk down their hard-earned dough for that first novel — and all the novels that have followed — I wouldn't be able to avoid honest labor and work the greatest job in the world."[95]

• During the 19th century, composer Franz Liszt was a major celebrity, as is demonstrated by these anecdotes: 1) He used to go to fancy restaurants, order tea, and leave a few drops in the cup. Women fought each other for the privilege of drinking those drops. 2) After he had sat on a chair, an American woman took the covering off the chair, had the covering framed, then hung it on a wall. 3) An old woman who smelled of tobacco even though she never smoked admitted that she had acquired a stub of a cigar that Liszt had smoked and was carrying it around in her corset.[96]

Food

• As of late 2010, New Zealand taxi driver Daniel Chung had been serving the homeless a Sunday lunch at his own expense for three years. He started after hearing that some homeless people in his Christchurch, New Zealand, community had died while sleeping outdoors. Each week, he spends between $100 and $300 (New Zealand Dollars) to feed the homeless. He also supports a wife and four children; his family helps serve the meals. Mr. Chung had been a chemical engineer in South Korea, but after moving to New Zealand, he was unable to find a job in chemical engineering, so he started to drive a taxi. He says, "A couple of years ago I heard two people died during the night. One of them here [in Latimer Square]. I thought he was homeless, so I started here. I had it in my heart to help them — I had to." His mother, a pastor in South Korea, was an inspiration to him. Garry Dickey, who has been homeless for 26 years, was one of the first people to be fed by Mr. Chung. Mr. Dickey remembers, "I was minding my own business. It was a nice sunny day, and he came over and said, 'Would you like a feed?' He told me then that he would come back every Sunday." The first time Mr. Chung fed the homeless, he brought a bag of burgers. But more and more homeless people began to show up, so he needed to bring more and more food. He admits, "It is a struggle financially to keep doing it," but he adds, "If possible, if God permitted me, I would do this to the end of my days. It's an eternal job I will do until I leave this world."[97]

• A Quaker preacher named John Parker once stopped at a hotel, where he was seated at a dinner table with two other preachers who were not Quakers. A waiter appeared at their table and left a dish on which were two fish. Each of the other two preachers took a fish and put it on his plate, and then they bowed their heads in prayer. As they were praying, Mr. Parker took the two fish from off their plates and returned them to the serving plate. After the two preachers had said their prayer, Mr. Parker told them, "Friends, my religion teaches me to watch, as well as to pray. We shall now cut the fish into three parts."[98]

• Servers can be overly friendly. A waiter once asked an elderly Peg Bracken and one of her elderly female friends, "And what will you have, young ladies?" Ms. Bracken's elderly female friend gave the waiter a one-finger salute. At another restaurant, Ms. Bracken overheard a headwaiter tell a busboy, "Take care of the dandelions in the corner, OK?" Ms. Bracken looked and saw six white-haired old ladies, who did look like dandelions whose seeds were about to be scattered by the wind.[99]

• French operatic bass Pol Plançon enjoyed rich food, but as he grew older, people worried that his taste for rich food might harm his operatic voice. When Italian baritone Antonio Scotti approached him with this fear, Mr. Plançon replied, "My dear friend, I shall live but once. And I can pay no higher tribute to life than to enjoy to the full all the fine things it has to offer."[100]

Chapter 3: From Friends to Mishaps

Friends

• Puff Daddy was best friends with Biggie Smalls, aka the Notorious B.I.G., who was murdered. After Biggie had been shot several times, Puffy and a friend rushed him to a hospital, where he died. Puffy said afterward, "I want to make sure that Biggie's name goes down in history with some positivity." He and Biggie's ex-wife, whose name is Faith Evans, recorded "I'll be Missing You," a tribute to Biggie that reached number one on the charts. Puffy made $3 million from the song — money that he used to set up a trust fund for Biggie's two children: Christopher and T'yanna. Biggie had recorded his albums with Puffy's recording company, and Puffy used his own share of the profits from Biggie's posthumously released *Life After Death* to do such good deeds as fund community programs, including Daddy's House, where Puffy says that city children can receive "positive experiences — computer camps, summer camps, boys' and girls' clubs, ethics classes. ... I've gotten where I've gotten because I had a chance to dream, and I want to instill that in kids. All kids have a spark in them. Somebody just needs to ignite that spark. They can accomplish anything."[101]

• In 1930, Arturo Toscanini conducted *Tannhaüser* at the Bayreuth Festival, held in Bavaria. At intermission, several people waited to see Maestro Toscanini, including King Ferdinand of Bulgaria and Princess Margherita. However, the Maestro chose to see only a couple of old friends, ignoring the royalty. Afterward, he was asked if he had been aware that royalty had wished to see him. He replied, "Yes, yes, they told me. But what have I to do with kings and princesses? They have nothing to say to me. I have nothing to say to them."[102]

• Italian baritone Titta Ruffo and Italian tenor Enrico Caruso were friends. According to one story, while Mr. Ruffo was attending a performance by Mr. Caruso, he was asked his opinion of Mr. Caruso. Mr. Ruffo replied, "He's magnificent — he scares me." A few days later, while Mr. Caruso was attending a performance by Mr. Ruffo, he was asked his opinion of Mr. Ruffo. Mr. Caruso replied, "He's magnificent — he scares me."[103]

• Geraldine Farrar and Enrico Caruso were great friends, and Ms. Farrar confided in him her fears about failure. Mr. Caruso encouraged her and predicted, "Farrar *fara*" — "Farrar will succeed." She liked the motto so much that she used it on a seal for her letters.[104]

Good Deeds

• A woman was shopping at her local supermarket, but when she went to pay for her groceries, she had lost the $200 she had been carrying with her. The woman at the checkout counter suggested that she go to the courtesy counter to see if anyone had handed in the money, but she laughed and said, "Really? It's cash — no one would hand that in!" The woman went to her truck to get some money that was intended to pay for other things. She paid for the groceries, and again the woman at the checkout counter suggested that she go to the courtesy counter to see if anyone had handed in the money; after all, she said, "You never know." The woman who had lost the money did go to the courtesy counter and ask if anyone had found and turned in two $100 bills. Someone had. Who? The woman at the courtesy counter pointed to a 10-year-old girl who was standing nearby with her mother. The woman who had lost the money hugged the mother, who said, "It wasn't me; it was my daughter." The woman who had lost the money replied, "I know, I wanted to thank you both, although she found it ... it's because of you that I got this back." Later, a friend gave the woman who had lost the money five tickets to a circus. She went back to the supermarket and the courtesy counter to ask the woman there if she knew the girl who had found and turned in her money because she wanted to give that girl and her family five tickets to the circus. The woman at the courtesy counter did. In addition, the woman who had lost the money said, "She told me that the family of the little girl who found my money don't have very much, so they would really appreciate this. She also said that they have three children, so five was the perfect number of tickets!" By the way, the woman who had lost the money wrote about this story online at Dailygood.org. She signed herself "Oneluckylady." She concluded her essay by writing, "At first, I had felt a little weird bringing those tickets to the store but I am SO glad I did! Lesson: Never think twice about doing something nice for someone."[105]

• In 2000, Kevyn Aucoin did the make-up for Hilary Swank at the Academy Awards; she won the Best Actress Oscar for *Boys Don't Cry*. (The previous year, he did the make-up for Gwyneth Paltrow at the Academy Awards; she won the Best Actress Oscar for *Shakespeare in Love*.) Actually, the production company of *Boys Don't Cry* could not afford Mr. Aucoin's very expensive thousands-of-dollars fee, but in *Boys Don't Cry*, Ms. Swank played a transgendered teen. Mr. Aucoin, a gay man, was so impressed by the movie and so impressed by Ms. Swank that he did her makeup for free. Mr. Aucoin was an activist in many ways, and he admired other activists. Mary Tyler Moore requested that he do her makeup for a public-service announcement for juvenile diabetes. He did her makeup for free, impressing Ms. Moore, who said, "I suspect that Kevyn helped every human being he came in contact with feel better about life and themselves." Movie-star Sharon Stone is active in raising money to fight AIDS, and Mr. Aucoin offered to do her makeup for free when she appeared in events for AmFAR, aka the American Foundation for AIDS Research. This impressed Ms. Stone, who said, "Let me ask you, who gives anything away for free?" He also did her makeup when she married — on Valentine's Day — newspaper executive Phil Bronstein. Kevyn was born on Valentine's Day, so Sharon brought out a 36th birthday cake for him and then brought out a wedding cake. By the way, the late Mr. Aucoin was very capable of playing a joke on a famous friend. While a camera was filming his technique as he prepared to put makeup on Kate Moss backstage at a fashion show, he announced to the camera, "I'm not going to give Kate foundation. I'm just going to put on a little bit of concealer, just light makeup, only where she needs it." Then he slathered concealer all over Kate's face until she looked like a geisha. She laughed. Also, please note that Kevyn once said, "Everyone has the potential to look beautiful."[106]

• In 1950, the grandparents of Matt L'Italien got married. They were David Rosenthal, a psychologist, and Marcia Kensinger Rosenthal, a nurse. Mr. L'Italien said, "My grandfather was Jewish and she was not, so it made things pretty difficult for them to get together." Mr. and Mrs. Rosenthal were in love, and they wrote two love songs together. They were married for 46 years before Mr. Rosenthal died of Alzheimer's in 1996. Mrs. Rosenthal died of the same disease a few years later. Matt's aunt, Amy Rosenthal, discovered an old love letter between the couple. She also discovered the piano sheet music and lyrics of the two love songs the two had written together: "In and Out of Love" and "I'll Never Regret (Loving You)." Unfortunately, no one in the family had the musical skills needed to play the music, so Matt posted the sheet music and lyrics, as well as a plea for help, at the Reddit online community. Matt said, "Reddit really is a place of benevolence. They actively want to help their fellow man." He wrote online, "My family recently found two songs on sheet music written by my late grandparents. Would anyone like to play them for us, so that we may hear them?" Quickly, he received several responses. Some people posted instrumental versions of the two songs, other people sang the two songs without accompaniment, and other people posted versions of the songs with both vocals and accompaniment. Matt, who never knew his grandfather, said about his grandmother, "I'm really happy that I can look back at this music she produced and really bring back that element of character and wit and brilliance that she had." He added, "My aunt who had the sheet music, it's her birthday, and she said it was the best birthday she could ever imagine."[107]

• Henry Rollins journeyed to Southern Sudan in late 2010. About visiting Africa, he writes, "Time spent there forces me to deal with myself on a level that is so in-your-face as it were, that I am always humbled. Anything I have ever strived for seems to be dwarfed by the efforts of people I encounter there in a seemingly endless succession." One example occurred on a bad road when he saw a woman carrying a large, heavy bag of cotton on her back while pushing a bicycle that had a flat tire as a result of an accident. Henry and the people he was with stopped the truck they were in to try to help her. Two of her toes were injured — badly. Mr. Rollins writes, "One of them looked almost cut off behind the cuticle and downward in a very ugly wound. The other toe had lost a fair chunk of flesh at its tip." They treated her with a first-aid kit and with Neosporin and gave her a pair of socks that she could wear over the bandages. Mr. Rollins also gave her the tube of Neosporin and told her to apply it to her wounds every day. They also took her and her bag of cotton and her bike to her destination, which was a long way away. They also learned that she would make that journey several times that day. Mr. Rollins says, "Just another day and another life in Africa. You see this kind of thing everywhere you look. When I am in Africa, I realize I don't know much, have not seen much and there's a lot to be done."[108]

• When the Germans defeated France (temporarily) in World War II, lots of Jews went to Bordeaux, where they hoped to find passage away from France before the Nazis arrived and took them to concentration camps. The ship *Kilissi* arrived in port with a cargo of bananas, and the captain was astonished to see 600 people, all of whom were begging to be taken away before the Germans arrived. The captain of the *Kilissi* spoke to his crew, asking them whether they were willing to risk their lives in trying to save the Jews on shore. Every member of the crew was willing. The crew then dumped most of the bananas overboard, since they had no time to unload them. The Jews crowded on board, and the *Kilissi* started to sail them to freedom. Almost immediately, however, the ship's engines stopped. Fortunately, the ship had stopped only to allow on board two men and one woman who were in a rowboat and screaming to get the ship's attention. The ship took the Jews to Portugal, but authorities there would not allow the Jews to disembark. However, the Jews were allowed to get aboard a French warship that was going to Morocco. Terry Wolf was one of the 600 Jews saved by the captain and his crew. She calls him "a gallant man to whom the value of human life meant more than bananas, profit, comfort, and personal safety. Whenever his final voyage, I hope it is to Paradise."[109]

• On 25 April 1989, at St. Anne's Catholic School in Fayetteville, North Carolina, Carl Boney and Michael Etowski, who were both 14 years old, climbed aboard the school bus. Things happened as usual for a while, but the bus driver, Richard Perry, suffered a stroke and slumped over. With no one steering the school bus, it went off the road and toward a utility pole. Mike said later, "I saw blue sparks and heard all this popping sound. I was slammed around. Then I jumped on the seat so I wouldn't get shocked. Everyone was freaking out. I looked up front. It didn't look like anyone was sitting in the driver's seat." Once past the utility pole, the bus headed for some trees. Carl, an African-American, went to the front and stepped on the brake, but he needed help because Mr. Perry's foot was still on the gas. Mike reached the front and helped Carl. Mike managed to turn off the ignition, and the bus came to a stop. Mike used his Boy Scout training to open Mr. Perry's airway and keep it open until paramedics arrived. Unfortunately, Mr. Perry died later in a hospital. According to Mike, "We're just ordinary boys." Carl added, "What we did was natural." Because of these two boys' actions, no kids were hurt on the bus.[110]

• Grammy nominee violinist Philippe Quint was seriously worried when he left a 285-year-old 1723 Kiesewetter Stradivarius violin — loaned to him by owners Clement and Karen Arrison — in the back seat of a New York taxicab on 21 April 2008. Fortunately, the driver of the taxi — Mohammed Khalil, a Muslim who was born in Egypt

— contacted him and returned the violin. Mr. Quint said, "I cannot describe it in words, the feeling that I was going through at the time. I was frantically looking for the violin that whole morning." Mr. Quint gave Mr. Khalil a $100 reward, performed a 30-minute concert for Mr. Khalil and other taxi drivers at Newark Liberty International Airport, which is only 15 miles from Midtown Manhattan, and gave Mr. Khalil and his family tickets to one of his concerts at Carnegie Hall. In addition, the city of Newark gave Mr. Khalil a medal. The Italian Antonio Stradivari made the violin, which has been owned by the 18th-century German composer and violinist Christophe Kiesewetter. Mr. Khalil said that he was simply doing the right thing in returning the violin.[111]

• In December of 2010 in Dayton, Ohio, police officer Jonathan Seiter stopped a man for a routine traffic violation, and the man started to attack him. Officer Seiter was unable to draw his gun, and the situation was dangerous. Angela Pierce, an African-American, was in a car with an elderly aunt, and she jumped out of the car and started punching the attacker with her fists. She later told CNN, "I didn't even think about what [the suspect] could have had. I didn't think about what he could have done to me. I just went and tried to help." With her help, and with the help of police backup in the form of Ohio Highway Patrol Sgt. Chris Colbert, who arrived after Ms. Pierce, Officer Seiter was able to subdue the attacker. Usually, ordinary citizens should not get involved in altercations between police officers and other people, but in this case Ms. Pierce did the right thing. Sgt. Larry Tolpin of the Dayton Police Department said, "Don't get me wrong, I'm not endorsing that citizens participate in this manner. But under this particular circumstance, it was very commendable of her."[112]

• In January 2011, Eva Orchard of Clearfield, Utah, experienced car trouble while driving on a cold mountain road. Because she knew little about cars and had no cell phone with her, she simply waited in her car and hoped that someone would stop and help her. Fortunately, after 20 minutes, a kind man named Bill stopped. Investigating the source of the car trouble, he thought that she had a faulty fuel pump. He had a cell phone, so he called AAA to come and tow the car, and he called Ms. Orchard's daughter. After the AAA tow truck arrived, Bill drove Ms. Orchard to where her car was being towed. He also declined payment for having helped her. In a letter to the editor of the *Standard-Examiner*, Ms. Orchard wrote, "I want everyone to know there are some really good Samaritans out there. I thank Bill for stopping and for all he did to see that I was well taken care of on such a cold morning."[113]

• In September of 2010, a taxi driver in Thailand found US$6,500 and Bt26,000 that a passenger had left behind. Duan Sosarn, age 34, whose right hand had been amputated, is an honest taxi driver. He took the money to Police Radio FM 91, which then located the passenger who had lost the money: Myo Htut, from Burma. Mr. Sosarn said that he wanted to be a good example to his son and that keeping the money would have been wrong. The police gave Mr. Sosarn a shield of honor on October 13, which is National Police Day in Thailand.[114]

• Rabbi Shlomo Carlebach celebrated Purim in 1963 in grand style. Flush with money from a standing-room-only concert the previous night, he hired a small truck and a driver, and then went to three stores — a wine shop, a pastry shop, and a grocery shop — where he bought out the entire inventory of each of the three stores. After the truck was fully loaded, he started to make deliveries of *shalach monos* (gift baskets for the needy) to families throughout Jerusalem.[115]

• In Beverly Cleary's novel *Ramona Quimby, Age 8*, the Quimby family eats in a restaurant and an elderly gentleman compliments them by saying that they look like a "happy family," and then without their knowledge he pays for their meal. Something similar happened to Ms. Cleary in real life. She and her family were eating in a Mexican restaurant, and when it was time to pay the bill, they discovered that an elderly gentleman had already paid their bill because they were "such a nice family."[116]

• While making a recording, Enrico Caruso was not satisfied with his singing of "*Cujus Amimam*" from Rossini's *Stabat Mater*, so he sang it over and over until he was satisfied. After the recording was finally finished, he removed a pearl stickpin from his tie and gave the stickpin to the exhausted trumpet player, saying, "You merit reward. In the end I thought you also would crack."[117]

• Pope John XXIII was working late one night when he remembered that some guards had been posted outside his door to protect him. He opened his door and sent the guards home, saying, "It would be better for you both to be home in bed. Better to go to sleep. You don't need to watch over me — I'm protected by the Holy Spirit."[118]

Grandparents

• Peg Bracken's grandfather was a kindly man. For one thing, he was a generous tooth fairy, giving 50 cents for a tooth when 50 cents was worth something. He also wrapped the 50-cent piece in a note with invisible writing; the note contained a tooth joke such as this one: "How do you say farewell to a tooth? Bye, Cuspid." He was sympathetic when Peg volunteered to give a speech when she was in the 7th grade, only to discover that she was unable to write and deliver a good speech. In fact, she was so miserable about giving her speech that she vomited in front of him the day before she had to give the speech. He asked her to pray, and the next morning lots of snow had fallen — but not enough to result in her being unable to give the speech. Peg and her grandfather went out to the barn so she could practice her speech, and frost covered everything, including the keyhole. When her grandfather got out his key to unlock the door to the barn, he suggested to Peg that she lick the frost off the keyhole. The frost was pretty, and her family sometimes made delicious ice cream from snow, so Peg tried to lick off the frost, but her tongue froze to the keyhole. Trying to get her tongue loose, she yanked her head back and tore some skin from her tongue. Eventually, with the help of some warm water, she got loose, but her tongue became so swollen that she could not talk and therefore could not give her speech. Peg sometimes wonders if her grandfather knew what would happen when she tried to lick the frost from the keyhole. By the way, many years later Peg was supposed to introduce someone on a public occasion, but because of stage fright she froze at the podium, was unable to speak, and had to be led gently away.[119]

Halloween

• Not everyone understands kids. For example, in Beverly Hills the actor Robert Young, star of the TV series *Father Knows Best* and *Marcus Welby, M.D.*, used to give trick-or-treating kids on Halloween autographed photographs of himself — and no candy. One of the trick-or-treating kids was Marlo Thomas, future star of TV's *That Girl*. She says that the kids knew exactly how to respond to being deprived of candy — they soaped Mr. Young's windows.[120]

Hanukkah

• Walter Adler, his girlfriend (Maria Parsheva), and two friends were on a subway car when someone wished them "Merry Christmas." A Jew, he responded, "Happy Hanukkah." This was enough for some anti-Semites to start a fight. One rolled up his sleeve to show a tattoo of Christ. Mr. Adler says that the man said, "Happy Hanukkah, that's when the Jews killed Jesus." Ms. Parsheva said, "They just came at us so fast. The first thing that came into my mind was, 'Yeah, this is going to be violent.'" Approximately 14 people taunted the small group of four, calling them "dirty Jews" and "Jew b*tches." During the fight, Mr. Adler's nose was broken and his lip was busted. One person who came to his aid was a Muslim from Bangladesh named Hassan Askari. Mr. Adler said, "A random Muslim guy jumped in and helped a Jewish guy on Hanukkah — that's a miracle." Mr. Adler pulled the emergency cord, and police arrested 10 people. Mr. Askari, a modest hero who ended up with two black eyes, said, "I just did what I had to do. My parents raised me that way." Mr. Adler invited Mr. Askari to celebrate Hanukkah with him; Mr. Askari accepted the invitation. According to a post on the Web site The Muslim Workplace, "Please note that Hassan Askari is not the exception among Muslims worldwide. He is what all Muslims are expected to be, and he behaved in the manner that all Muslims are expected to behave when they see a fellow human being needing help." The following January both Mr. Adler and Ms. Parsheva attended an appreciation dinner given to honor Mr. Askari by the Islamic Circle of North America, which in a written statement said, "Mr. Askari embodies the principles of courage, strength and love for fellow Americans as taught by the Quran and Sunnah."[121]

Heroes

• In April 2010, 7th-graders Allyson Golden and Miriam Starobin laughed at something funny that their music teacher, Sanford Mauskopf, said at Long Beach (New York) Middle School. Allyson said, "I was chewing gum, which I shouldn't. I was laughing hysterically and suddenly I realized I'm not laughing any more. I can't breathe. Then Miriam goes, 'Ally, are you choking?' I can't speak. So my arms are around my neck. I'm turning purple, and my legs are flailing." Allyson was frightened when she was unable to breathe; she said that "it was the scariest moment of my life. I was thinking 'I'm going to die. What will my parents think?'" Fortunately Miriam knew exactly what to do — a result, she thinks, of remembering a SpongeBob SquarePants cartoon that she had seen on Nickelodeon. Miriam said, "It was like a flash right in my eyes. I saw in my head Squidward with his clarinet lodged in his throat and then SpongeBob does the Heimlich maneuver and the clarinet comes flying out of his mouth. I had no clue what I was doing until it was done." Miriam performed the Heimlich maneuver on Allyson, and the gum popped out of her mouth. Immediately afterward, Allyson gave Miriam "the biggest hug" and said to her, "Miriam, you just saved my life. I owe you big time." Miriam replied, "Oh, no, no, you don't. It's no big deal." Their music teacher, Mr.

Mauskopf, did not see Allyson choking because his view was blocked, but he did see the gum flying through the air. He asked the girls, "What's going on?" After learning what Miriam had done, he said to her, "Do you realize what you've just done? You've saved Allyson's life. You're a hero." (By the way, a Nickelodeon spokeswoman later said that actually SpongeBob did not perform the Heimlich maneuver on Squidward; therefore, Miriam may be conflating the cartoon with a demonstration of the Heimlich maneuver that she saw elsewhere. Whatever. Miriam saved Allyson's life, and that is the important thing.)[122]

• One of the heroes of the 2007 Virginia Tech shooting was Waleed Shaalan, a 32-year-old engineering graduate student and Muslim who came to the United States from northern Egypt. Randy Dymond, a civil engineering professor at Virginia Tech, said that an email from a student who wished to be anonymous, but who was in the same room with Mr. Shaalan when the gunman attacked, told the story of Mr. Shaalan's heroism. Mr. Shaalan was badly wounded, but the student who later emailed Mr. Dymond was unharmed and played dead as he lay by Mr. Shaalan. The gunman left the room but later returned and looked around. Just as the gunman was about to discover the unharmed student, Mr. Shaalan deliberately attracted the gunman's attention. The gunman shot and murdered Mr. Shaalan, and he left the room, leaving the unharmed student alone. Mr. Dymond says that the anonymous student wanted the story to be known "so that the family of Waleed understands the sacrifice." Hearing Mr. Dymond's account of Mr. Shaalan's last moments of life, Mr. Shaalan's mother said, "He was trying to save someone else." At Virginia Tech, Mr. Shaalan was active in the Muslim Student Association.[123]

• In 1986, the Crites family took off in a Cessna 172 airplane from Banff National Park in Canada. However, the winds were high and the airplane crashed in a stream soon after takeoff. Dr. Darrell Crites, who was piloting, and his wife, Gloria, were killed instantly. Their two daughters, six-year-old Tammy and 11-year-old Korrina, were still alive. Korrina was badly injured with a broken jawbone, wrist, and cheekbone and fractured skull; Tammy had a broken collarbone. Korrina could barely move, so Tammy used luggage to float Korrina to shore. Korrina could not move any further, so Tammy set out to find help. She walked through the woods, shouting for help. Three women hikers heard her, but they couldn't find her, so they telephoned Scott Ward, the park warden, who used a helicopter to find Tammy, who then led him to Korrina. Mr. Ward said later, "When the plane crashed, her father's body was lying on top of Korrina. Apparently, Tammy pulled her sister out from under her father, got her up onto the creek bank and then headed off for help. Isn't that something for a 6 1/2-year-old girl?"[124]

• On Friday, 4 February 2011, a mentally ill Hispanic man started stalking Sabrina Scott, an African-American single mother in a New York subway. Ms. Scott said, "I tried to get away, and he started chasing me. I panicked." As he chased her, the mentally ill man hissed, "Are you scared of me?" Ms. Scott cried out for help, which arrived in the form of a tall African-American man wearing a baseball cap and headphones. As the two men fought, Ms. Scott fell onto the subway tracks. When she regained consciousness, paramedics were taking care of her. The Good Samaritan who had come to her aid had chased off the mentally ill man and then had gotten Ms. Scott off the subway tracks before he himself left. While recovering in the Bellevue Hospital Intensive Care Ward with a concussion and a dislocated thumb, Ms. Scott said, "I want to say thank you to whoever it was. I have a son that I need to be here for, so thank God I'm still alive. Thank God." Ms. Scott's father, Ben, said about the Good Samaritan, "He really saved my daughter. We're all so glad that no train was coming. That would have been devastating." Constance Zuniga, Ms. Scott's sister, added, "We'd like to thank him personally and take him out to dinner."[125]

• In April 2008, a school bus driver left the bus to go to the restroom, and the bus started rolling down a hill. (It is against the law for a school bus driver to leave unattended a bus with schoolchildren on board.) David Murphy, an African-American 5th grader, became a hero. He said on *Good Morning America*, "The bus had started rolling. Then there was a truck in front of it, and I looked up and it was rolling. Then I decided to get in front of the wheel to turn it from the truck." He steered the bus, which was filled with children, away from the truck. The bus hit the pillar of a bridge and stopped. Brian Seitz, a lawyer and family friend of the Murphys, said on *Good Morning America*, "David is absolutely the most modest hero I've ever met, but [if not] for his actions, that bus would have went right down into the river. He saved all of those children's lives. I think it has yet to really sink in. He's very, very modest. I want to commend him. I've known the family for quite some time. But [if not] for his action, 26 of his classmates and possibly his own life would have possibly — could have been a horrible tragedy."[126]

Husbands and Wives

• Stephen King used to listen to music while he wrote, but he has stopped doing that. Why? He says that "frankly my brains used to work better than they do now." However, his wife may have had something to do with it. He used to listen to a tape of "Mambo No. 5" by Lou Bega (sample lyric: "A little bit of Monica in my life, a little bit of Erica by my side") over and over and over. One day his wife came into his study and told him, "Steve, one more time ... you die!"[127]

• Jacques Offenbach, the composer of many famous overtures, occasionally forgot to button the fly of his pants, so his wife developed a code phrase to remind him of this necessary social duty. If they were at a party, and she began to speak about "Monsieur Durand," Offenbach knew that he needed to get away somewhere private so he could button his pants.[128]

• Art Linkletter is famous in part because of his interviews with children. For example, he asked a small girl what she wanted to be when she grew up. She replied, "An airline stewardess. My aunt was one, and she told me you can marry rich millionaires." When Mr. Linkletter asked her whom her aunt had married, she answered, "The airport janitor."[129]

• Wolfgang Amadeus Mozart's widow, Constanze, defended his memory. She once was offended by a book by Friedrich Schlichtegroll about her deceased husband, so she bought up all the copies of the book and removed the passages she didn't like.[130]

Illnesses and Injuries

• In his old age, Pierre-Auguste Renoir was crippled by rheumatoid arthritis, but he continued to paint. Unable to walk, he was either carried in a sedan chair or pushed in a wheelchair. His hands were twisted, and according to his son Jean, "Visitors who weren't used to it couldn't take their eyes off the mutilation. Their reaction, which they didn't dare express, was 'It's not possible. With those hands, he can't paint these paintings. There's a mystery!'" According to Jean, "The mystery was Renoir himself." In order for Mr. Renoir to paint, a piece of cloth was pushed into the center of his hand, which was like a claw, and then a brush was pushed into his hand. A mechanism was created in order to move large paintings so that the part that Mr. Renoir wanted to work on was within his reach. With these adaptations, Mr. Renoir was able to continue to create masterpieces despite his infirmity. In 1919, his last year of life, Mr. Renoir painted both *Girl with a Mandolin* and *The Concert*, although he looked like a skeleton and his voice was so weak that people could barely hear him.[131]

• A man became obsessed with a woman, and he convinced his doctors that he would die unless he could sleep with her. However, the sages of the community said, "Let him die rather than have her yield." The doctors then asked that the woman stand naked before the man in order to save his life, but the sages said, "Let him die rather than that she stand naked before him." The doctors then asked that the woman talk to the man while standing behind a fence in order that his life be saved, but the sages said, "Let him die rather than that she talk to him behind a fence." In other words, according to this story from the Babylonian Talmud, *Sanhedrin* 75a, if a man becomes obsessed with a woman, that's his problem — she is not required to help him.[132]

• In 1951, renowned conductor Herbert von Karajan prepared to make a recording of Bach's *B minor Mass*. He rehearsed the Gesellschaft der Musikfreunde chorus and the Vienna Symphony 70 times to prepare for the recording, but he came down with a case of blood poisoning two days before the first recording session. Nevertheless, he conducted from a stretcher, raising one arm into the air, and the recording was outstanding.[133]

• When George Plimpton attended Cambridge, he got sick. Unfortunately, the housekeeper talked to him for a very long time. Growing tired, he wanted her to leave, and trying to be polite, he said to her, "I must ask you to leave now. My favorite radio program is just coming on." As she was leaving, George turned on the radio, only to hear the announcer say, "Come now, children, clap your hands!"[134]

Insults

• Luigi Cherubini once insulted Hector Berlioz, who got his revenge at a performance of Cherubini's *Ali Baba*. Berlioz sat in a front seat at the opera and yawned. Loudly he said, "I'll give 20 francs for one musical idea." Later he said, "I'll give 40 francs for one musical idea." As the opera progressed, Berlioz kept raising the price he would give for the presence of a musical idea in the opera, and then finally he left, saying, "I give up. I'm simply not rich enough."[135]

• At one time, wealthy amateur conductors could hire famous orchestras and conduct them. One such conductor hired the Vienna Philharmonic, which is composed of truly professional musicians. Unfortunately, this amateur conductor decided to show off, so he lectured the Philharmonic about how to play music. This was and is not wise. The musicians of the Philharmonic got their revenge by following the amateur conductor's beat.[136]

• Opera singer Nellie Melba could be very rude. Once, she and Mary Garden were invited to give a concert at Windsor Castle for the King of Greece. At the supper following the concert, Ms. Melba said, "What a dreadful concert this would have been if I hadn't come!" Lord Farquhar started to compliment Ms. Garden, but she said simply, "Please don't bother about me, Lord Farquhar. I love Melba's rudeness. It amuses me."[137]

Language

• Yankee pitcher Lefty Gomez frequently came off the pitcher mound to complain to umpires. During one game, he complained too often to umpire Harry Geisel, who told him, "One more time, Lefty, and you're outta here!" Sure enough, a few pitches later Lefty came off the pitcher's mound, and Mr. Geisel thought that he would have to throw him out, but Lefty said, "I didn't come down here to argue about that pitch, Mr. Geisel. I just wanted to ask you how you spell your name. The umpire replied, "G-E-I-S-E-L." Lefty then said, "That's just what I thought — one eye."[138]

• John Dexter used to produce operas in Paris, although he spoke English and a young woman would translate his comments so that other people could understand them. Occasionally, Mr. Dexter would become really angry and curse people in English, and the young woman would diplomatically translate his comments. However, Mr. Dexter knew enough French to be aware of what the young woman was doing, so he would order her, "Tell them what I *really* said."[139]

• With the heavily accented Georg Solti as conductor, the Chicago Symphony Orchestra recorded Benjamin Britton's *Young Person's Guide to the Orchestra*. Maestro Solti was supposed to later record the narration in several languages: English, French, German, and Italian. However, one day he announced to the orchestra that the recording would not appear for sale. Why? He joked, "No one can understand me in any language!"[140]

• Baseball manager Casey Stengel was known for speaking Stengelese, which occasionally sounded like sensible speech but often was not. Following an interview with Mr. Stengel, Joe McGuff, a sports reporter, asked Ernest Mehl, a sports editor, "What did he say?" Mr. Mehl replied, "I haven't the faintest idea, but it must be a heck of a story, and I'm going to write it."[141]

• Ludwig van Beethoven was capable of making good puns and of giving credit where is due. After hearing an overture by Carl Maria von Weber, he said, "*S'ist eben gewebt*" or, in English, "It is nicely woven." ("Weber" means "weaver.")[142]

Makeup

• Kevyn Aucoin had adventures in makeup even before becoming a rich and famous Hollywood makeup artist. 1) When he was in the 7th grade, a friend named Michelle came to class with new and interesting eyes that sparkled and glistened. He was amazed and asked, "What did you do to your eyes?" She replied, "I plucked my eyelashes." He thought that if that had worked for her, it would surely work for him, so he plucked a few eyelashes with painful and swollen results. Of course, he soon realized that Michelle had plucked her eye*brows*, not eye*lashes*. 2) When he was even younger, he and his brother often played outside and got mosquito bites, resulting in the application of an anti-itch calamine lotion that dried into a cakey paste with a whitish-pink color. When his mother took him shopping for school clothes, young Kevyn saw a woman who seemed as if she had been bitten by many mosquitoes and had to smear calamine lotion all over her face. He said, "Ma'am, look! My legs have calamine lotion all over them, too!" His mother hushed him and took him outside, where she explained that the woman had been wearing foundation makeup, not calamine lotion. As an adult, Kevyn realized that the choices in makeup in 1967 were quite limited. 3) The adult Kevyn learned that applying liquid eyeliner to your own eyes can be quite difficult. He once tried to teach his mother to do that with the result that she used up a large bottle of makeup remover. Actually, the two — mother and son — used up two large bottles of makeup remover. Kevyn was used to applying liquid eyeliner to other people's eyes, and he did not believe that applying it to your own eyes would be difficult, so his mother made him try to apply it to his own eyes. 4) The very young Kevyn once got into the family medicine cabinet in search of his mother's orange lipstick, which he thought would taste like candy. He took a bite and discovered that it did not taste like candy, then he tried to give the lipstick the shape it had had before he took a bite out of it. The lipstick ended up in one hand, and the lipstick tube ended up in another hand. One thing led to another, and the adult Kevyn wished that he had a photograph of his mother when she walked into the bathroom and discovered that everything was orange.[143]

Media

• Not all interviewers are as prepared as they think they are. James Marshall, who wrote and illustrated a series of children's books about two characters named George and Martha, once was interviewed by a woman on a radio show in Chicago. Before the interview, he asked her, "Do you need any information about myself?" She replied, "No. I've done my homework." Unfortunately, her first question to him on the air was, "What's it like writing about the First Family?" Mr. Marshall replied, "Well, it's not that George and Martha." She then asked, "Who are they, then?" Mr. Marshall replied, "Well ... they're hippos." As you may expect, the interviewer was completely unprepared to interview him, and Mr. Marshall had to take over the interview.[144]

• Lynne Taylor Corbett was present at a press conference when fellow choreographer Alvin Ailey was asked, "Do you prefer to be called black or negro?" He replied, "I prefer to be called Alvin Ailey, choreographer."[145]

Mishaps

• When she was a student nurse, Ethel Gillette went to a hospital for her first clinical. She took care of a patient, and all went well until the patient said, "I want my robe, please." Three robes were hanging in the closet, but the patient said, "No, dear — I want the blue one I had on before my bath. It's my favorite because it's the last gift my niece gave me. She was killed in an automobile accident a year ago." Ms. Gillette thought, and she realized that she had gathered the blue robe along with the bed sheets and she had put everything down a laundry chute. She also knew that the bleach used at the hospital would ruin the robe. She said, "Would you excuse me, please?" Then she went to her instructor and asked to take a break. Just by looking at her, her instructor knew that something was wrong, and she asked, "Gillette, what did you do?" Ms. Gillette explained the situation, and her instructor said, "All right — run. Find the nearest stairway and run down to the basement." It took her a while to find the laundry room, and it was filled with soiled linen, but she realized that it would be impossible to replace the blue robe because of its sentimental value. She kept opening up bags of soiled linen, and each time she opened up five bags of soiled linen, she thought to herself, *Just five more, and I'll quit.* The 35th bag of soiled linen held the blue robe. She took it back to the patient's room and laundered it by hand and hung it over a towel rack to dry. She writes, "I went back in [the patient's room], explained what had happened and we both had a good laugh; hers from amusement, mine from relief."[146]

• Late one afternoon movie critic Roger Ebert walked across London's Hyde Park from Kensington Gardens to Hyde Park Corner. Unfortunately, the gates of Hyde Park are locked at dusk as he discovered when he found himself locked inside the park that rainy winter evening. He climbed up a muddy hill, falling twice and getting himself muddy, and he reached a tree that he climbed in an attempt to get to the top of the iron fence. He climbed from the tree to the top of the fence, but the jump down was too unsafe for him to attempt without help. Fortunately, an American boy, who was with friends, saw him: "Hey, look, it's Roger Ebert! No way! Is that really you?" Mr. Ebert assured the boy that in fact he was Roger Ebert, and he admits that in the situation he was in, "If I had been the Queen, I would have answered to Roger Ebert." The American boy replied, "Far out, dude! What are you doing up there?" Mr. Ebert answered truthfully, "Trying to get down." The American boy and his friends helped him down, and Mr. Ebert gave them his autograph, then he returned to his hotel and enjoyed a fire and a hot bath.[147]

• When Jon Scieszka, who would later be an author of books for young people, was a kid, he and his older brother Jim often got in trouble. For example, their mother told them not to wrestle in the living room because they would break something. Ignoring her warning, they wrestled in the living room, and they broke the front two legs of the couch. Jon was plenty worried about what would happen when their mother found out, but Jim said, "Don't worry. I know exactly what to say." Their mother found out, and she asked them, "What happened to the couch?" Jim replied, "Jon did it." Jim and Jon shared a bedroom in the basement, which sometimes got cold, so they sometimes used an electric heater. One day they got the idea that they could put out the electric heater the same way that they put out campfires — by peeing on it. The air filled with a nasty odor of fried urine, and they unplugged the heater and opened the windows wide on a freezing day. Jon says, "And whenever our mom asked us about the heater, we said we didn't really need it anymore."[148]

• As a student at the School of American Ballet, Merrill Ashley was able to buy at a low price toe shoes that had been rejected by members of the New York City Ballet. She purchased a pair of toe shoes that had been rejected by Allegra Kent, who had small, narrow feet like Merrill's. She got them ready for a performance at a workshop, tying ribbons to them, and then put them away. Unfortunately, at the time of the performance, she discovered that the shoes were too small

— her feet had either grown bigger or had swollen from the hours of lessons and rehearsals. Since they were the only toe shoes she had ready, she crammed them on her feet and danced — earning herself many, many blisters. Still, the pain was worthwhile because dance critic Clive Barnes singled her out for praise in *The New York Times*, writing, "And one dancer with promise was Linda Merrill." (This was before she changed her name to Merrill Ashley.)[149]

• Pope John Paul II, nee Karol Wojtyla, was active in outdoor sports as a young man. When he was a Cardinal, he skied too near the Czechoslovakian border, and a military patrol stopped him. Cardinal Wojtyla showed him his papers, but the Communist soldier told him he was in big trouble: "Do you realize, you moron, whose personal papers you have stolen? This trick will put you inside [prison] for a long time." Cardinal Wojtyla spent a long time persuading the soldier that the papers were authentic because the soldier kept telling him, "A skiing Cardinal? Do you think I'm nuts?"[150]

• At one time, pulpits were custom built to suit the height of the local preacher. This could lead to problems when guest preachers stood up to preach. Foy E. Wallace, Jr., was a short guest preacher at a Church of Christ, but the regular preacher, Rube Porter, was over six feet tall. When preacher Wallace stood in back of the podium, no one could see him, so he said, "If you don't see me anymore, remember that 'faith comes by hearing,' Romans 10:17."[151]

Chapter 4: From Money to Prayer

Money

• In order for Milton Ochieng' to go to the United States to attend college, he needed money. He got it: His neighbors in the Kenyan village (with a population of about 1,100 people in 2008) known as Lwala sold chickens and cattle to raise $900 for his plane ticket to the United States, where Mr. Ochieng' attended and graduated from Dartmouth College and then attended and graduated from Vanderbilt University Medical School. His brother, Fred, followed him to the United States. Together, they raised $150,000 to build a health clinic in Lwala. The Blood:Water Mission, a Nashville, Tennessee-based nonprofit that was founded by Christian rockers Jars of Clay, contributed money to help build the clinic. Its program director, Barak Bruerd, says, "It's not common to have a couple of village boys come to the U.S. and advocate for a clinic to be built in their country. The fact that they were able to bring so much support to their community is amazing." Dr. Milton Ochieng' remembers that when he was young he saw ill people being pushed in wheelbarrows to reach a paved road they could travel on to get medical treatment. In Africa, the American dollar goes far. In its first year of existence, the clinic treated 20,000 patients. Cost: just under $100,000. Dr. Milton Ochieng' says, "There's such a sense of love and people feeling they've gained so much from the health center. It keeps me going. ... It makes you realize how great it is to be a doctor, how great it is to be serving humanity." The clinic is named the Erastus Ochieng' Lwala Community Memorial Health Center in honor of the brothers' father.[152]

• Sometimes it takes an older relative to teach a kid morality. When Ed Burke was a kid growing up in Chicago, he got a job mopping a small grocery store owned by an elderly black couple at the end of each workday. They kept their money in the bottom of a flour barrel in the back, and they were forgetful and did not keep good records, and so

Ed figured that he could take a little money each night and they would not miss it. Therefore, he would reach down into the barrel each night and take some change or a bill or two, never looking to see what he had pulled out because he was so afraid of being caught. He then would put the money in the trashcan, take the trash out, and then take out the money from the trash can. One night, he pulled out two bills, and when he looked at them after taking out the trash, he was shocked to see that they were $20 bills — $40 was a lot of money in the 1920s. He was scared to have that much money on him because if people saw it, they would figure out that he must have gotten it illegally, but he was greedy enough that he did not want to return the money. Therefore, he rented a safe deposit box and put the money in it. A year later, the bill for the safe deposit box rental came to his house, and his aunt got it. Curious, she found out why Ed had a safe deposit box. She did a lot of yelling, she walked her nephew to the bank to take out all the money, and she walked him to the elderly black couple whose money it was and made him return it.[153]

• In 2008, New Zealand bus driver Nomeneta Tuaitau, a Samoan father of two, found a wallet with over $500 in it. He tracked down the owner and returned the wallet and money, and he declined to accept a reward, saying, "I have my family, and I have enough money. I've worked as a bus driver for three years, and I enjoy it because I can serve the public." The wallet's owner, an English tourist named David Procter, was happy to receive the wallet and the money, especially since he needed the money to do a good deed of his own while visiting Auckland. Mr. Procter said, "I came here on an emergency trip to help an old friend. He is totally blind and deaf and had hit a few hard times. When I got here, he had been made homeless. But we've now found him a place to live — he's back on his feet, and he can rebuild his life. It has been a successful trip, and without Nomeneta's help it would have been really difficult for me to do this." Mr. Procter said about Mr. Nomeneta, "This act is heroic. Nomeneta didn't just hand the wallet in as lost property. He took the time to make sure I was okay, and [he] didn't want any reward." Mr. Procter loves New Zealand and says, "Escaping the English winter is one reason, but I also love the space, the scenery, and the Kiwi attitude to life. If I was 20 years younger, I would have moved here."[154]

• Rabbi Shimon was once asked to address a gathering of rich men, but he agreed only on condition that he be lent 50,000 rubles the day before his address, to be repaid the day after his address. Because Rabbi Shimon was known to be an honest man, this condition was readily agreed to. When Rabbi Shimon gave his address, he spoke eloquently on the evils of the love of money, and many rich men in the audience felt compelled to improve their ways of doing business. The day after his address, Rabbi Shimon, as he had promised, repaid the 50,000 rubles. The people who had lent him the money noticed that the Rabbi was returning the same bills that he had been lent, and they wondered why he had borrowed the money since he had not used it to buy anything. Rabbi Shimon explained that he had borrowed the money because poor people were often intimidated by rich people, but because of the 50,000 rubles he had borrowed, he did not feel poor and so was able to criticize the sins of the rich people in the audience.[155]

• People sin, but they can repent. For example, someone stole a hammer decades ago from Central Contractors Supply Co. in western Pennsylvania. Eventually, the thief repented and sent an envelope containing money and a note to the owners — the Gramling family — of the supply store. The note stated that the writer had stolen a hammer from the family-owned supply store 25 or 30 years ago. The note also stated, "I knew it was wrong, but I did it anyway. Enclosed is $45 to cover the hammer plus a little extra for interest. I'm sorry I stole it, but have changed my ways." Lots of things have been stolen from the store over the decades, said co-owner Lynne Gramling, but this was the first time that a thief paid for what was stolen. She took the money to her father, also a co-owner of the store. He was ringing a bell for the

Salvation Army, and she put the money in his kettle. She said that the money was "really a lot more than a hammer would cost. He was very generous."[156]

• A man lived near Rabbi Zusya. Because the Rabbi was very poor, the man gave him money each day so that the Rabbi could buy the necessities of life for himself and his family. Because of this, God rewarded the man handsomely. The man then thought, If God rewards me handsomely for what I give to Rabbi Zusya, wouldn't God reward me even more if I were to give money to Rabbi Zusya's master, who is an even better man than Rabbi Zusya? The man gave money to Rabbi Zusya's master, but the man then suffered financial misfortunes. Therefore, the man went to Rabbi Zusya and asked why this had happened. Rabbi Zusya answered, "As long as you gave to those who had need, and did not worry about their worth, God did the same. But when you sought to give only to those who were worthy, God did the same."[157]

• During an audience that Pope John XXIII gave to several priests, he noticed one German priest who stood out because of his excellent clothing. As he discovered through the priest's answers to his questions, the priest came from a diocese of millionaires. As the two men talked, the priest volunteered information about how he was able to coax the rich people in his diocese to give generously during the collection at Mass. Before each collection, the priest always said, "When the basket goes around, I don't want to hear any clinking, only rustling." This information made Pope John XXIII sad. He told the well-dressed priest, "Do you know, dear friend, that when poor men sacrifice a coin of theirs, that a part of their heart goes into the collection basket with it? ... That's the reason I would rather hear clinking."[158]

• One day, Nasrudin saw a beggar who asked him for money. When Nasrudin asked what the beggar needed the money for, the beggar replied that he wanted money to buy himself new clothing, to take his friends to a good restaurant for a good meal, and to finish the evening by taking his friends to a coffeehouse. Therefore, Nasrudin gave the beggar a coin of great value. Soon, another beggar came to Nasrudin and asked for money. When Nasrudin asked this beggar what he needed the money for, the beggar replied that he wanted to buy some bread and cheese. Nasrudin asked whether the beggar wanted some new clothing and to treat his friends to food and coffee, but the beggar replied that he had simple tastes and spent most of his time praying. Therefore, Nasrudin gave this man a coin of small value.[159]

• Dr. Alfred G. Robyn, the noted Bach authority, composer, organist, and pianist, once went to a dentist for bridge work. The dentist was pleased to discover that his patient was a famous pianist and asked him to serve as accompanist for a series of recitals at which he — the dentist — was singing. Dr. Robyn agreed, but he was surprised when, after the recitals, the dentist sent him a bill for the dental work, itemizing such tasks as "examining teeth, cleaning teeth, preparing teeth," and so on. In response, Dr. Robyn sent the dentist his own bill, itemizing such tasks as "opening piano lid, putting music on rack, playing on black keys, playing on white keys, closing piano lid," and so on. Finally, Dr. Robyn compared the two bills — the dentist's and his own — and added this P.S.: "You owe me fifty cents."[160]

• A Rabbi who was very critical of the rich used to tell this story. When Moses came down from Mount Sinai, he was carrying the two tablets on which the Ten Commandments had been engraved, but when he saw the Israelites worshipping the Golden Calf, he broke the tablets. Because the tablets were decorated with costly jewels, the rich grabbed the largest pieces of the tablets, while the poor — crowded out by the rich — grabbed the smallest pieces. When they looked at their pieces of the tablets, the rich read, "Thou shalt ... murder" and "Thou shalt ... commit adultery." However, on their pieces of the tablets, the poor read, "not ... not ... not." That is why the rich can get away with everything, while the poor are allowed to do nothing.[161]

• A wealthy merchant once offered a dervish a thousand pieces of gold; however, the dervish asked the merchant questions before accepting the money. The dervish asked if the merchant had more money at home. The merchant answered yes. The dervish then asked if the merchant wanted twice as much as the amount of money he already had. Again the merchant answered yes, adding that every day he prayed to God to give him more money. Hearing that, the dervish said, "I can't accept your money because a rich man can't accept from a beggar. I am rich because I am satisfied with what God gives me, while you are poor because you are always begging God to give you more."[162]

• During bull markets, baseball players often become fascinated with the stock market, and back when railroads were a major means of passenger travel manager Casey Stengel was pestered by players asking him for stock-market tips. The fascination with the stock market was keeping the players from being fascinated with baseball, so after a pitiful practice Mr. Stengel called a team meeting and informed his players that he had a stock-market tip for them: "Buy railroad stock. I'm going to [fire and] ship out so many of you guys that the railroads are bound to increase their profits."[163]

• Musician James Chance once performed in New York in a club that the Mafia owned. After the performance, he asked for his pay, but the Mafia told him to f**k off. Mr. Chance then took out a knife and the Mafia guys took out their guns because they were worried that he was going to attack them. However, Mr. Chance did not attack them. Instead, he started cutting his own arm. The Mafia guys freaked out, threw his money at him, and yelled, "GET OUT OF HERE!"[164]

• Even early in his career, conductor Leonard Bernstein could be outspoken. After hearing a politician congratulate the city of New York for supporting such a fine organization as the New York City Symphony Orchestra, Mr. Bernstein yelled, "FRAUD!" He then explained that New York City did not contribute even a penny toward paying the orchestra's bills.[165]

• Al Capp became successful with the comic-strip *Li'l Abner*. In fact, the comic strip was immediately popular and so the *Boston Globe* published an article about him. This did have one unforeseen result, however — all the art schools that Mr. Capp had studied at sent him bills for his unpaid tuition! (He paid them all.)[166]

• A few days before he died in July of 1833, William Wilberforce was made immensely happy because England decided to free its slaves. "Thank God," he said, "that I have been suffered to live to see this day when England is ready to sacrifice twenty millions of pounds sterling [in payments to slave-owners] to emancipate her slaves!"[167]

Music

• Some people who hear punk music think that it is created by no-talent musicians who can't even tune their guitars. Sometimes, they are right. One of the punk singers with no discernible talent was a nutter named Jon the Postman because his name was Jon and he was a postman. According to punk critic Steven Wells, "He got on stage and screamed his way through whatever song came into his head. He had no discernable talent whatsoever, but he didn't give a f**k. To many, Jon the Postman symbolized what punk was all about." What does that mean? It means that punk is all about doing it — now. If you wait to get on stage until you're good enough to get on stage, you might never get on stage. So get on stage. Mr. Wells writes, "Jon the Postman did it. He got on stage, and he put out records. And everyone who ever saw him perform or listened to his music laughed like a drain. And then thought — 'F**k! If *he* can do it, so can I.' Jon the Postman wasn't anybody special. He was just a postman called Jon. But in 1976 and 1977 he lived his life as if he were a superstar. Jon the Postman WAS punk rock."[168]

• Ian Svenonius, a member of the Washington, D.C., punk bank Nation of Ulysses, was once named Sassiest Boy in America by *Sassy*, a magazine for North American teenage girls. As his reward, he stayed two days in New York City, hung out with *Sassy* staff, got a Magic

8 Ball, and was allowed to take what he wanted of *Sassy*'s collection of CDs that the staff did not want. *Sassy* writer Christina Kelly mentioned to Ian's friend Calvin Johnson that she thought that Chia Pet would be a good name for a band, and Calvin told her that she should start a band with that name. The following week she received a phone call from Calvin telling her that Chia Pet had a gig opening at Bard College for Ian's Nation of Ulysses and for Beat Happening (Calvin's own band). Christina rose to the challenge. She and some other *Sassy* employees and friends started the band Chia Pet and played. Calvin had not told Bard College anything about Chia Pet except that they were a New York band, and people at Bard College were excited when they recognized the *Sassy* employees in Chia Pet.[169]

• Henry Rollins had some interesting and weird experiences as lead singer of hardcore group Black Flag. Sometimes, the band would go such long distances to get to their next gig that band members peed out the window rather than stop at a gas station. Sometimes, Mr. Rollins would go outside on a break from performing and find it hard to get back in to perform because the bouncer didn't think that he was in the band. Once, while in Minneapolis, Minnesota, he went to a used record store and heard a man tell a woman, "This place is great! I found the first Black Flag album for three bucks last week!" The woman replied, "Three bucks? I'll give you mine for free." And once he attended a Grateful Dead concert that he enjoyed very much — even the police officers were enjoying themselves and throwing Frisbees. One police officer looked at Mr. Rollins and said, "Nice tattoos. If you ever get bored, you can read yourself."[170]

• Soprano Frances Alda gave many concerts throughout the United States during her life, and sometimes she ran into travel problems. Once, a blizzard kept her from reaching a destination in time for a concert, and since she knew she could not sing on the day she was scheduled, she telegraphed to say that she would sing the following day, which happened to be Sunday. This shocked a local clergyman, who wrote to the town newspaper that holding a concert on Sunday was a sin. Ms. Alda also wrote a letter to the town newspaper to say that she also preferred to rest one day out of seven. However, she added, if God had to choose between the singing at the clergyman's church and the singing at her concert, there wouldn't be much difference — unless God truly had a musical ear, in which case He was much more likely to choose her concert.[171]

• Conductor Arturo Toscanini never gave encores. While giving the first performance of *Euryanthe* by Carl Maria von Weber, Toscanini was at first pleased by the applause of the audience following the overture. However, the audience kept applauding and demanding an encore. For 10 minutes, Toscanini stood with his back to the audience, and he grew angrier and angrier because he wished to proceed with the performance. Finally, he turned around, screamed "No *bis* [encore]" to the audience, broke his baton and threw the pieces at the audience, then left the stage. The première was postponed until the following week.[172]

• When Ignaz Joseph Pleyel came to Vienna from Paris, his newest string quartets were played at Prince Lobkowitz's. Beethoven was in the audience, and after the string quartets were played, he was asked to play. After being coaxed for a long time, he finally consented angrily, and sat at the piano with the music from the second violin part of one of Pleyel's quartets in front of him. He improvised for a long time, using the notes of the music of the second violin, and when he was finished, an astonished Pleyel kissed his hands.[173]

• At one time, opera/lieder singer Kathleen Ferrier had trouble producing a top A note. Therefore, for one of her performances at Glyndebourne, Benjamin Britten wrote for her an F sharp instead of a top A. However, during her performance he was startled when she produced the top A. Later, she confessed that she had gotten excited and forgotten about the F sharp. After that performance, she continued to sing the top A.[174]

• The night before the premiere of *Don Giovanni*, Wolfgang Amadeus Mozart was having a good time at a party when the conductor rushed in looking for him. "Where is the overture?" the conductor asked, anxious because so little time was left for rehearsing it. "Don't worry," Mozart said. "It's all up here, in my head." During the rest of the night, Mozart wrote out the overture and in the morning he gave it to the copyists. (Even so, the overture arrived at the theater only a half-hour before opening, and no time was left to rehearse it.)[175]

• Leopold Stokowski once surprised his Philadelphia Orchestra by meticulously rehearsing Johann Strauss' "Blue Danube" since it was not scheduled to be played at any concert that year. The mystery was explained when Maestro Stokowski was in the audience for a summer concert by the Philadelphia Orchestra, which was being guest conducted. Maestro Stokowski was asked to conduct something, and after making a pretense of reluctance, he conducted the orchestra in Strauss' "Blue Danube."[176]

• Otto Klemperer concentrated on the music while he was conducting. Once, he was conducting a Beethoven symphony at the Royal Festival Hall in London when his violinists noticed that the famous conductor's fly was undone. The first violinist attempted to get Mr. Klemperer's attention by rolling his eyes, and at a break in the music, Mr. Klemperer asked what was wrong. After hearing that his fly was undone, Mr. Klemperer merely asked, "What's that got to do with Beethoven?"[177]

• Feodor Chaliapin admired Enrico Caruso, and as a tribute to him, he once wrote a glowing appreciation on the walls of Mr. Caruso's dressing room at the Metropolitan Opera. Of course, this was greatly prized by the Metropolitan Opera, and for years the tribute was not touched — when the room had to be painted, the painters painted around the tribute.[178]

• Sir Thomas Beecham once had to cancel a week of rehearsals for a concert at which Brahms' Second Symphony would be played. This made a young musician nervous because, as he told Sir Thomas, he had never played Brahms' Second Symphony before. Unperturbed, Sir Thomas replied, "Then you'll just love it when you play it at the concert."[179]

• Mrs. Elizabeth Billington, a soprano, once received a wonderful compliment from Franz Haydn, who saw a painting that Joshua Reynolds had created of Mrs. Billington. Haydn told the painter, "You have made a mistake. You have represented Mrs. Billington listening to the angels; you should have made the angels listening to her."[180]

• The BBC Orchestra was and is composed of truly fine musicians. Once, Arturo Toscanini led them in a rehearsal of a new piece of music by Vincenzo Tommasini. The musicians sight-read the music so well that Mr. Toscanini, astonished, said to them, "I do not understand — how can you have seen this music before?"[181]

• Sir Thomas Beecham was a feisty conductor. When he was old, he conducted the Chicago Symphony Orchestra in Delius' "Brigg Fair," and he sang along with the orchestra. However, he heard the audience coughing, and he suddenly turned around and shouted, "Be quiet! I can't hear myself sing!"[182]

• In Richard Strauss' *Alpine* Symphony, a passage of music portrays a storm. During a rehearsal conducted by Mr. Strauss, the first violinist dropped his bow. Mr. Strauss stopped the rehearsal, saying, "Gentlemen, may we pause briefly? Our leader has lost his umbrella."[183]

• Ludwig van Beethoven once lived in a house on whose window shutters he made musical notations. After the famous composer moved out of the house, the landlord auctioned off the shutters.[184]

Names

• When Jon Scieszka, who would later be an author of books for young people, was in the 3rd grade at a Catholic school, he learned that his class could adopt a pagan baby from another country and give money so the child could grow up Catholic and get an education and have food, shelter, and clothing. As an incentive for the children to raise money for the pagan baby, Sister Mary Catherine announced that the boys would be pitted against the girls, and whichever group raised the most money would be able to name the baby. This motivated the boys, and they raised enough money for the class to adopt two pagan babies, surprising Sister Mary Catherine with their fundraising prowess. Now it was time to name the pagan babies. Sister Mary Catherine suggested, "The names of the apostles — Mathew, Mark, Luke, and John — are very nice." But the spokesboy for the boys said, "We've already decided on our names. We're going to name our pagan babies Al Kaline and Bill Freehan." Sister Mary Catherine objected, "But those aren't apostles." The spokesboy replied, "Heck, no. They're the best Detroit Tigers ever. Freehan will definitely hit .300 this year. And Kaline is gonna get 30 homers for sure." Sister Mary Catherine replied, "Matthew and Mark will be fine names." And those are the names that she wrote down for the pagan babies. With that, the boys lost interest in the contest, and thereafter the girls always won. Today, Jon knows that in the pagan parts of the world lots of guys are running around with the names Matthew, Mark, Luke, and John; however, he says, "There should be two guys with the coolest names ever. But we got robbed."[185]

• Light soprano and coloratura Natalie Dessay ran into voice problems. After discovering that she had a pseudocyst on one vocal cord and a polyp on the other, she underwent surgery — twice — to correct the problem. The operations worked. By the way, she is French but prefers "Natalie" to the French "Nathalie" in honor of Natalie Wood. In addition, she has named her three cats Cyst, Nodule, and Polyp.[186]

Old Age

• Quite a few people are surprised to see that they have grown old. Peg Bracken once walked into a store with her husband. She looked at the image on the closed-circuit television and thought, "That's a pleasant-looking old couple over there." Then she realized that she was looking at an image of herself and her husband. By the way, Peg once got two tickets to a fashion show and asked a friend to go with her. The friend declined, saying, "They make me feel old and ugly and fat and broke. Why do you go?" Peg replied, "It makes my feet feel good to watch the models teeter around in the high heels. I bet they can't wait to take them off." In her old age, Peg sometimes thought of what her last words should be. Her research on last words turned up her absolute favorite: Doris Medina, the mother of author John J. Medina, said, "Will you please turn off the television?"[187]

• Barbara Klassen's great-great uncle lived to be 106 years old. During that time, he was healthy and happy and he served as a chauffeur to help other old but less-healthy senior citizens get around. On his 100th birthday, his driver's license needed to be renewed, but a clerk asked him, "You're 100 years old. What do you need a driver's license for?" He answered, "Somebody has to drive the old folks around."[188]

• When cellist Pablo Casals was 95 years old, opera singer Plácido Domingo visited him. He was pleasantly surprised to find that Mr. Casals, despite his frail old age, was busy studying the score of Mendelssohn's *A Midsummer Night's Dream*.[189]

Parents

• Poet Wanda Coleman is African-American. In 1931, her father came to California after a young black man was lynched in Little Rock, Arkansas, where her father then lived. He simply offered some people driving through in a car that bore California license plates $15 to take him to California. Her mother worked as a housemaid and cleaned the home of Ronald Reagan when he and Jane Wyman were married. She asked him for a raise, he wouldn't give it to her, and so she quit. Wanda's parents then met in a church in California. Her father helped her to get an education. Whenever she went to her library, for some reason she was allowed to check out only books for girls, and she wanted to read books for boys. Therefore, she would go to the library with her father, she would pick out the books she wanted to read, and he would check them out for her.[190]

• In the summer of 1920, the parents of Dick King-Smith, the author of *Babe: The Gallant Pig*, met. Dick's father was on crutches, the result of an injury in World War II, and he noticed a pretty, 18-year-old woman. Shortly afterward, she was confined to her room with a cold. He found out where she was staying, and he went there and stood in the sand of the beach. He waited until she appeared at a window, and then he used a crutch to write in the sand, "GET WELL SOON."[191]

People with Handicaps

• Samuel Long's parents can hear, but he is deaf. His parents taught him sign language in addition to all the other things that parents teach their children, including colors. When he was young, his mother would ask him in sign language what color something was. If he answered correctly, she would sign to him, "Good boy, Sam." One day, when the Long family was painting the house, Sam disappeared for a short time. When he returned, he was completely naked, except for a coating of green paint. He signed to his mother, "What color, Mom?" She signed back, "Green." He replied in sign language, "Good girl, Mom." He wanted to be like the other kids, so he got headphones, and he pretended that he could listen to music in the headphones. One day, he and his mother were in a store; he was wearing his headphones, and his mother was speaking to him in sign language. The saleslady assumed that his mother must be the deaf one, so she began writing a note to her. After all, what would a deaf kid be doing with headphones?[192]

• Philadelphia Phillie Dick Sisler stuttered, and he took a lot of good-natured ribbing from opposing players. Since he had been a Navy chief petty officer, players often asked him, "Whatta ya say,

"Ch-ch-ch-ch-Chief?" Mr. Sisler always replied, "Fa-fa-fa-fa-fine, thanks." One day, a lost stranger asked for directions, saying, "Hey, bu-bu-bu-bu-buddy, where's fo-fo-fo-fo-forty-second street?" Mr. Sisler says, "I was af-af-af-af-afraid to answer."[193]

Pranks and Practical Jokes

• Eric Carle, author and illustrator of the children's book *The Very Hungry Caterpillar*, loves animals. When he was young, his grandparents kept a few animals in back of their factory, which was located next to their home. One of the animals was a goat that used to visit Eric's grandmother, whom Eric called Oma. The goat climbed up three flights of stairs in her home and then butted her door with his head so she would open the door and give him a treat such as a handful of oats. Eric's grandparents also kept chickens. Eric knew something about chickens, and although he loved his grandmother, he was not above playing a trick on her. He gently took a chicken and put it on its back, holding its body and its head down for 30 seconds. When he released the chicken, it lay there quietly. According to the adult Eric, "Thousands of years ago when chickens still lived in the wild, they 'played dead' in order to fool a fox or weasel about to attack." Eric did this to four chickens in all, and then he rang the bell to his grandmother's room. When she looked out the window, he pretended to be greatly excited and pointed to the chickens, which looked as if they were dead. His grandmother came running, and when she reached the chickens Eric clapped his hands and the startled chickens jumped up and began to act the way live chickens act. His grandmother then took Eric by the ear and marched him to her kitchen — but Eric was not punished. Instead, she made him hot cocoa and fed him a cookie she had made from scratch. Eric says, "You can see why my Oma was special."[194]

• In the late 1970s, the Pail & Shovel Party, which became known for its art projects, aka wacky pranks, led the student body of the University of Wisconsin. In 1979, they made it seem as if the Statue of

Liberty were located in the nearby, frozen Lake Mendota by placing on the ice of the lake a replica of the top half of the Statue of Liberty's head and the arm holding the torch. Also in 1979, they planted 1,008 plastic pink flamingoes on the front lawn of Bascom Hill, a campus landmark. Flamingo-planting became and remains a University of Wisconsin campus tradition.[195]

• Sol Hess, the cartoonist of the long-ago comic strip *The Nebbs*, once returned home late and noticed that a neighbor's window was covered with newspapers — the neighbor had taped them to the window to protect his privacy after sending out the drapes to be cleaned. Mr. Hess telephoned his neighbor and requested that the neighbor turn the pages and retape the newspapers to the window because he had already read the pages that faced the street.[196]

• Comedian Jonathan Winters and his friends will sometimes put on the people around them. In a crowded elevator, he once asked fellow comedian Pat McCormick, "You don't think we tied him up too tight?" And in a crowded hotel lobby, he once told a friend, "We never should have operated in a hotel room. Granted, he's alive but you shouldn't have let the brain fall on the rug. Next time, St. Vincent's [Hospital]."[197]

Prayer

• A pious man once went to say his prayers at a mosque. However, an uneducated man was already saying his prayers there, and the uneducated man mispronounced a word of his prayers. The pious man felt that it would be inappropriate to stand near the uneducated man to say his prayers, so he moved away from the uneducated man before saying his prayers. That night, the pious man dreamed that God spoke to him, saying, "If you had stood behind the uneducated man and said your prayers, you would have earned My pleasure. Instead, you found fault with his pronunciation, and you ignored the purity and excellence of his heart. I cherish a pure and excellent heart much more than the correct pronunciation of words."[198]

• On Rosh Hashanah, the Jewish New Year, God passes judgment upon people — either for life or for death. One year, Rosh Hashanah fell on the Sabbath. Rabbi Levi Itzchok prayed, "Master of the World, Thou knowest that today is not only the first of the year but also the holy Sabbath. Since Thou hast ordained that no writing be done on this day Thou too will not desecrate this day. It is therefore impossible for Thee to inscribe our verdict for the coming year without violating the Sabbath. There is only one thing that Thou art able to do. Thou mayest insert the word 'life' for all of us since Thy sacred law teaches that the saving of life alone permits the violation of the Sabbath."[199]

• Children sometimes say funny things in prayers. A nine-year-old once prayed, "Please bless dad's family jewels." A three-year-old whose father pretended that the long cardboard tube from a roll of wrapping paper was a sword prayed, "Please bless me that I can smash daddy's sword into tiny pieces." A three-year-old girl prayed to thank God for letting her "play in the middle of the night." Often, her parents found her awake and playing after 10 p.m.[200]

• Once, the originator of Hassidism — the Baal Shem Tov, also known as the Besht — declined to enter a house of worship. When asked why, he said, "The prayers recited here were uttered in a lifeless and mechanical manner. They had no wings. They never reached the higher spheres. They are choking the House of God. There is no room for me."[201]

• One day, Edwin Porter, a preacher, was playing with his little granddaughter and saying things like, "Throw the ball to Grandfather" and "Walk for Grandfather." After playing like this for some time, the call for breakfast came, and Rev. Porter prayed over the morning meal, "Our Grandfather in Heaven, we thank thee ...."[202]

Chapter 5: From Preachers to Zen

Preachers

• The evaluation committee of Rev. J. Christy Ramsey, the pastor of the Ottawa (Ohio) Presbyterian Church, once gave him the humbling task of comparing his own ministry to that of Jesus. Rev. Ramsey came up with many observations, including these: Jesus walks on water; Rev. Ramsey slips on ice. Jesus changes water into wine; Rev. Ramsey changes water into coffee. Jesus curses fig tree; Rev. Ramsey kills houseplants. Jesus raises the dead; Rev. Ramsey wakes teenagers. Jesus casts out demons; Rev. Ramsey turns on night-light. And finally: Jesus cleanses lepers; Rev. Ramsey has changed dirty diapers.[203]

• John Bright's speeches could be understood by everyone in the audience. Before speaking in public, Mr. Bright tested his speeches on his gardener. If the gardener was unable to understand the speech, Mr. Bright changed the speech until the gardener was able to understand it. A famous passage written by Mr. Bright concerned the Crimean War: "The angel of death is abroad in the land; you can almost hear the beating of his wings."[204]

Problem-Solving

• In 1988 in West Seneca, New York, 12-year-old James Bliemeister ran into a problem when the three-year-old child he was babysitting caused a gas leak by ramming his pedal-powered fire engine into a gas pipe. Gas began hissing out of the hole, and James covered the hole with his finger. A gas leak can be dangerous because of the dangers both of suffocation and of an explosion. He knew that a pack of chewing gum was upstairs, and he sent the three-year-old to get it. Unfortunately, the three-year-old brought him some toy cars, so James sent the three-year-old upstairs again. When the child returned with the gum, James chewed several pieces and used the gum to plug the hole in the gas pipe. He then tied a sock around the hole so that the gum and sock would continue to stop the gas leak. James next telephoned his father, and his father telephoned the gas company. No suffocation. No explosion. One hero.[205]

• Sherri Jean Phelps, a teacher in the San Francisco Bay area, ran into a problem with a young Korean-American student named Young. He was a very good student, but the crossing guard complained that Young would sometimes risk his youthful life by running into traffic when the crossing sign clearly said, "DON'T WALK." Ms. Phelps talked to Young and discovered that he knew how to read the words "WALK" and "DON'T WALK," as she expected he did. He even demonstrated what the word "WALK" meant by walking. However, when she asked him to explain the meaning of "DON'T WALK," he replied, "Sign say, 'DON'T WALK,' so I run." Of course, she explained that "DON'T WALK" means to stand still and wait for the sign to change to "WALK." Problem solved.[206]

• Soprano Frances Alda once was scheduled to give a concert at Versailles in the home of the Marquise de Brou. However, the audience was very noisy, and so she did not start singing even when her accompanist began to play. The Marquise asked her what was the matter, and Ms. Alda replied, "I know I am supposed to have a very strong voice, but even so it would be impossible for me to make myself heard above all this *tohu-bohu*." This shocked the audience into silence, and she sang without distractions. By the way, Mary Garden once told Ms. Alda, "I am always having to explain you to people. Half of them think you're a grand person, and the rest think you're a b*tch." Ms. Alda replied, "They're both right."[207]

• Kathleen Engle, a middle-school physical-education teacher in Newcastle, Wyoming, is famous there for her toe talks. When kids are mean to each other, sometimes without realizing it, she makes the kids touch their toes when she lectures them "about their behavior, how it looks to others, and whether they realize what they're doing." Why make the kids touch their toes? She explains, "Because they're staring at their toes, they can't play off of each other with the rolled eyes and the shrugs and touching each other. Because when they're looking at each other, they're not listening to me." This really works. She says, "Often kids will come to me and say, 'I didn't really realize what I was doing.'"[208]

• Architect Frank Gehry was Jewish, and when he was serving in the US Army from 1954 to 1956, he occasionally ran into anti-Semitism. One Army sergeant called him by the slur "Kikey." Mr. Gehry complained to his company's commanding officer, who brushed off his complaint. Later, he complained to some officers he knew at the service club, and one officer told him, "Don't worry about it. Give me his name." Mr. Gehry did, and within three days the anti-Semitic sergeant learned that he had been transferred — to Alaska. When the sergeant told Mr. Gehry the news, Mr. Gehry replied, "I'm sure you'll find lots of kikes up there."[209]

• As a girl, Moravian soprano Maria Jeritza was sent to a convent because her mother wanted her to take the veil, but Maria decided against it when she learned that her long hair would be cut short. Therefore, to get out of the convent, she made use of the rule that any novice would be dismissed whom the Mother Superior had reprimanded three times. To get her three reprimands, Maria performed these actions: during a time of prayer, she sewed the habits of two novices together; she stole fruit from the garden next door after climbing over the wall; and she crashed a domino board over the head of an opposing player.[210]

• Dick King-Smith, the author of *Babe: The Gallant Pig*, had a chance to be a TV personality on a children's show called *Rub-a-Dub-Tub*, on each episode of which he presented a segment about animals. However, he was stiff the first time he tried to speak to the metal box that was the TV camera. Fortunately, Anne Wood, the producer of the show, asked him, "Who's your youngest grandchild?" The answer was Charlie, and Anne told Dick, "Just imagine that Charlie is inside that metal box. Talk to him as if he were." This worked, and Mr. King-Smith started sounding much more like his natural self.[211]

• A mother once asked Manuel Garcia, a noted voice teacher, to take her daughter as a pupil. However, Mr. Garcia knew that the daughter was not suited to be one of his pupils, so he asked the mother and daughter to attend one of his lessons. At the lesson, he made a voice student practice difficult passages over and over, and the mother and daughter soon looked at each other, horrified, then left. As they left, the daughter told the voice student, "That would kill me." Mr. Garcia complimented the voice student who had been practicing the difficult passages, then continued with his normal lesson.[212]

• Sir Hamilton Harty was conducting Brahms' Second Piano Concerto when pianist Artur Schnabel's memory failed him. Sir Hamilton recognized the error immediately, and he held up both hands. One hand made the sign for "2," and the other hand made a slashing motion across his throat. The well-educated Hallé orchestra cut two bars of the music, and the audience did not detect Mr. Schnabel's lapse of memory. Afterward, Mr. Schnabel told Sir Hamilton, "The Hallé is nearly as good as the Berlin Philharmonic." Sir Hamilton replied, "They're better — two bars better."[213]

• Cromwell Barnard was both a Quaker and the captain of a ship. Once, his ship was at a certain wharf, and the officer of a rival ship decided that his ship would take the place of the good Quaker's ship. Captain Barnard protested, but the rival officer would not listen to him. Therefore, Captain Barnard called to his first mate, who was a non-Quaker, and told him, "Mate, I think thee'll have to come up here and use some of thy language." The first mate hurled a volley of oaths at the rival officer, and the rival officer decided to let Captain Barnard's ship alone.[214]

• Early in her career, while she still was in Athens, Greece, Maria Callas sang the lead in *Tosca* with Antonis Thellentas (sometimes spelled Dellendas). Mr. Thellentas was popular with the Greek audience because of his voice, acting, and size, all of which were great. He had the reputation of being able to eat almost two pounds of macaroni at a single sitting, and because of his size Maria's mother writes that when he and Maria sang an impassioned duet together, she sometimes was forced to close her eyes.[215]

• Opera singer Ian Wallace recalls the time when a very heavy Italian soprano played the part of Gilda in *Rigoletto*. In this opera, Gilda is murdered, then carried off in a sack by the character Sparafucile. Unfortunately, the singer playing Sparafucile was unable to lift the singer playing Gilda, so the opera director invented three new characters — burly men all — to help Sparafucile lift and carry Gilda off the stage. (This story may be why Sir Rudolf Bing once wrote, "The greatest singers in the world don't fit easily into blue jeans.")[216]

• Adelina Patti, a celebrated diva, seldom showed up for rehearsals (she included a no-rehearsal clause in her contracts), so she often first met her singing co-stars on the stages of the opera house she was performing at the time. In a first-act trio featuring Ms. Patti, a baritone and a tenor, the baritone altered the words of the song he was singing on stage to ask her for an introduction. Ms. Patti being willing, the tenor sang the formal introductions.[217]

• According to an ancient Jewish tradition, a blessing must be chanted when the Sabbath candles are lit. A businesswoman was scrupulous about chanting the blessing, but one Friday she found that she would be unable to return home in time to observe the tradition. So the businesswoman called home and had her maid light the Sabbath candles, then hold the telephone receiver near the candles so she could chant the blessing.[218]

• Pope John XXIII regarded some old customs as nuisances, but having respect for tradition, he modified them instead of entirely doing away with them. He was embarrassed by his attendants' kneeling three times before him whenever they entered or departed from his presence, so he changed the custom so that they kneeled to him only once in the morning and once in the evening.[219]

• Tenor Enrico Caruso was multi-talented. At a performance of *Bohème*, the bass who was singing the part of Colline whispered to Mr. Caruso that he had lost his voice. Mr. Caruso whispered back for the bass to move his lips, then Mr. Caruso sang the part of the bass with his back to the audience so no one could see what he was doing.[220]

• Tenor Lauritz Melchior was a big man. Fellow opera singer Marjorie Lawrence writes that when he stayed at the Ansonia Hotel on Broadway, it did not have a bath big enough for him. Therefore, each morning he took the service elevator to the basement, where he dunked himself in the swimming pool.[221]

Rabbis

• R' Elya Chaim, the Rav of Lodz, discovered that a shopowner had been desecrating the Sabbath by opening up his shop on the holy day. Therefore, the good Rabbi rose on the Sabbath, sent a message to the synagogue that no one was to wait for him, then he went to the store and sat down in front of its door. The shopowner soon arrived, keys in hand and ready to open his shop for business. He saw the Rabbi, figured that he was waiting for someone, and decided to wait for the Rabbi to leave so he could open the shop. A couple of hours passed, and the shopowner finally realized what the Rabbi was doing, so he admitted defeat and told R' Elya Chaim, "Rebbe, I give up. Go home and eat. I swear by my wife and children that from now on my store will remain closed on Shabbos."[222]

• Rabbi Zushia of Hanipol never rebuked a sinner for sinning. Instead, when he saw a person commit a sin, he would sit near that person, then begin crying, "Zushia, how could you commit such a sin? Don't you know that you will have to account for that sin in the World-to-Come?" The sinner always listened to Zushia and eventually repented.[223]

Royalty and Aristocracy

• Prima donnas can be vigilant in the pursuit of what they regard as their rights. While traveling with Colonel James H. Mapleson (1830-1901) and his opera company, two prima donnas — Caroline Salla and Anna De Belocca — feuded over who would get the best suite at a hotel. The good Colonel solved the problem by having the hotel manager mention that an equally good suite — which had been reserved for Lady Spencer — existed upstairs. Ms. Belocca asked to see the reserved suite, and when the door was open, she ran inside and locked the door, telling the hotel manager to find another suite for Lady Spencer.[224]

• The Quakers used to be persecuted in the early years of the colonization of America; however, King Charles II ended the practice by sending a Quaker as his envoy to America. Quakers believe in the equality of Humankind, so they don't take their hats off before humans of high rank. The American Governor was so displeased by the Quaker's not taking his hat off that he knocked the hat to the ground. However, as soon as he learned that the Quaker was the envoy of the king, he hurriedly picked up the Quaker's hat — and took off his own.[225]

• Leo Slezak, the famous tenor, was disembarking from Vienna to go on tour with his opera company. As part of his luggage, he carried a stage prop — a jeweled crown (with fake jewels, of course) in a hatbox. At the border, the customs officer went through Slezak's luggage. When the officer saw the crown, he was startled, then bowed respectfully to Slezak, saying, "I trust your Highness will forgive my having inconvenienced you. Please pass, your Highness."[226]

• Mary Lidbetter was a very pretty Quaker woman. In Brighton, England, in 1797, she caught the eye of the Prince Regent, and he followed her and kissed her. She immediately slapped his face, and he thereafter left her alone.[227]

Signs

• As a sometimes traveler, Peg Bracken occasionally ran across interesting signs. In Manhattan, she saw trashcans bearing this sign: LITTERING IS FILTHY AND SELFISH SO DON'T DO IT. And she once saw a shop that displayed this sign: SHOPLIFTERS WILL BE HAPPILY BEATEN TO A PULP. By the way, when Peg was a kid, her mother found this note in her pocket (and saved it and showed it to her when Peg was an adult): LUCILE IS A DOP.[228]

• Composer Johannes Brahms had a big ego. While walking with his friend George Henschel, he saw a building bearing a commemorative plaque. Mr. Brahms said to Mr. Henschel, "The day after I die, they'll put up a sign on my house, too." Mr. Henschel joked, "Of course they will. It'll say, 'House to Rent.'"[229]

Thanksgiving

• When Sarah Dash was in the 2nd or 3rd grade, she sang for the first time in front of people: a Thanksgiving song. She had been ordered not to scratch, but little Sarah was itchy, so before singing, she told her audience, "They told me not to scratch, but before I start to sing, I'm gonna scratch." Her audience laughed, and she says, "I've been a clown ever since." Later, she sang in the group LaBelle.[230]

Travel

• Rabbi Shlomo Carlebach was on an airplane about to depart when an airline representative announced that two people with medical emergencies needed to be on the airplane. The airline representative then asked if anyone would voluntarily give up their seats and take a later flight: "Is there anyone here who is willing to extend themselves to help out these people?" Immediately, Rabbi Shlomo said, "I'm ready!" He said this even though he was probably more booked and busier than anyone else on the flight.[231]

• On a British airplane about to take off, a steward announced, "Passengers are warned to keep their safety belts fastened throughout the flight until otherwise advised, as the trip is likely to be bumpy." A worried elderly woman asked, "Is it going to be very bumpy?" The steward — who was very dignified — replied, "Madam, I said bumpy, not very bumpy."[232]

War

• At the 1936 Olympics, Jesse Owens failed twice to qualify for the finals in the long jump. He should have qualified easily, but he was now in the position of not making the finals if he were to fault one more time. Fortunately, his German competitor, Lutz Long, helped him by advising him by start his jump about a foot before the fault line — that way, he would not fault and should easily qualify. The advice worked, and Mr. Owens made the finals, where he and Mr. Long competed for the gold medal, with Mr. Owens finally winning while Mr. Long won the silver medal. The two men became friends, and they stayed friends, although Mr. Long fought for the Germans in World War II. On a battlefield, Mr. Long wrote Mr. Owens, "I hope we can always remain best of friends despite the differences between our countries." Not long after, Mr. Long died in battle. After the war was over, Mr. Long's son, 22-year-old Peter, wrote Mr. Owens to ask him to be his best man at his wedding: "Even though my father can't be here to be my best man, I know who he would want in his place. He would want you to take his place. And I do, too." Mr. Owens flew to Germany, and was Peter's best man.[233]

• The United States certainly gets into a lot of wars. Journalist and cartoonist Ted Rall once spoke with a British reporter who came up with an amusing idea for keeping the U.S. out of wars. The British reporter said, "If the average American cannot identify three cities in a country, the U.S. should not invade it." According to Mr. Rall, "Given that the average American doesn't know their state capital, much less three cities in, say, Canada, this would transform us into a pacifist society overnight." Of course, ignorance abounds, and not just among common American citizens. D-Day took place at Normandy, and the Allied forces brought tons of food for civilians because the Allied forces thought that food would be scarce in Normandy. Actually, Normandy had plenty of food, although other places in France had food shortages — Allied bombs had destroyed train lines that normally would have transported food out of Normandy to the rest of France. Military officials telegraphed Eisenhower: PLENTY OF FOOD. SEND SHOES."[234]

• Quakers tend to be pacifists. In 1854, Eli Jones, who was a Quaker, was appointed Major General of a division of Maine militia as a joke. Mr. Jones responded that if he were to accept the position of Major General, he would "give such orders as I think best. The first would be, 'Ground Arms!' The second would be, 'Right about face! Go, beat your swords into ploughshares and your spears into pruning-hooks, and learn war no more!'"[235]

• When the Nazis were ready to march into Athens, Greece, during World War II, people went shopping for necessities, emptying the food shops quickly because they knew that food would soon be scarce. In addition, writes Maria Callas' mother, who was there, "The beauty shops worked overtime, for when war threatens, most women decide to have their hair washed and curled before the shooting starts."[236]

• British anthropologist Bronislaw Malinowski (1884-1942) once spoke with a cannibal who was aware of the vast number of casualties in World War I. The cannibal asked how the Europeans were able to consume so much human flesh. Told that Europeans did not eat human flesh, the cannibal was horrified and asked how Europeans were able to kill human beings for no reason.[237]

Wisdom Stories

• Long ago, before Christ, a man traveled to the Han-ku Pass in northwest China. The Keeper of the Pass recognized the man and talked to him. The man was Lao-tzu, aka Old Master, and he planned on journeying into the wilderness and never returning. The Keeper of the Pass begged him to first write down some of his wisdom, and after thinking for a while, Lao-tzu agreed. He wrote a brief condensation of his wisdom on bamboo tablets, and then left, never to return. The bamboo tablets contained the *Tao Te Ching*, aka Tao Virtue Classic, and it speaks of Tao and its principles, the most important of which is to work with nature, not against it. This book did not remain static, for it has been interpreted and reinterpreted — the result of additional wisdom, as shown by the varying ancient texts that have come down to us. A famous passage from the *Tao Te Ching* is this: "A journey of a thousand miles begins with a single step."[238]

• A flood came and forced a man to climb out on his roof. A boat came to rescue him, but the man said, "I have faith that God will save me," so the boat went away. The water continued to climb until it reached the man's waist. Another boat came to rescue him, but the man said, "I have faith that God will save me," so the second boat went away. The water continued to climb until it reached the man's neck. A helicopter came to rescue him, but the man said, "I have faith that God will save me," so the helicopter went away. The water continued to rise, and the man drowned and went to Heaven. In Heaven, he told God, "I had faith that You would save me from drowning. I am surprised that I drowned." God replied, "I am also surprised that you drowned. After all, I sent two boats and a helicopter to save you."[239]

Work

• At a time when it was easy to find a job as a busboy, Taoist teacher Luke Chan got a job as a busboy. He wasn't making a lot of money, but he was able to afford to buy what he calls "a third-rate automobile." Often, he would pick up hitchhikers because he felt sorry for them because they could not afford a car. But one day a hitchhiker asked him for a dollar, and he thought a moment and realized that the only difference between him and the hitchhiker was that he was not lazy and that he worked. Thereafter, he picked up no more hitchhikers. According to Mr. Chan, "Laziness is a major cause of poverty in developed countries." Mr. Chan also tells this story: A rich man's son and a poor man's son had to choose careers. The poor man's son chose making furniture, but the rich man's son chose slaying dragons. Soon, the poor man's son was rich because many people needed furniture made, and the rich man's son was poor because no one needed a dragon slain. By the way, Mr. Chan says that modern universities have lots of classes about how to slay dragons. He then asks, "But if you had a choice, wouldn't you rather learn something practical rather than something that's merely theoretical?"[240]

• From her Paris teacher, Cécile Gilly, soprano Marjorie Lawrence learned that when asked if she knew a certain opera, she should always say that she knew it. That way, she would get more jobs; after all, she could always learn the opera after getting the job. Therefore, early in her career, when Ms. Lawrence was asked if she knew the *Tétralogie*, she replied that she did, although she had never heard of it. Later, when she met Ms. Gilly, she asked what the *Tétralogie* was, explaining that she had said that she knew it. Ms. Gilly laughed, then explained, "Do you realize, young woman, you told the man you knew the whole of Wagner's *Ring*? Here we call it the *Tétralogie*." Ms. Lawrence was kept quite busy learning the *Tétralogie*.[241]

• Gioacchino Rossini used to boast about his procrastinating abilities, which caused music managers to tear their hair as they waited for him to finish composing a piece of music. In a letter, Mr. Rossini boasted, "In Italy, in my time, all the managers were bald at thirty." For example, Mr. Rossini composed the overture to *Otello* only after being locked in a room with a little food while a manager waited for the music. While composing the overture to *La Gazza Ladra*, Mr. Rossini was watched by four men. These men took each page of the overture as it was written, then threw it to the copyists, who were waiting in a downstairs room. According to Mr. Rossini, the four men had orders to throw *him* downstairs if he failed to deliver the overture.[242]

• When author Lucy Grealy, author of *Autobiography of a Face*, was a skinny little girl, she used to work at a stable owned by a Mr. Evans in exchange for being able to ride the horses for free. She earned that right both for her work and for helping Mr. Evans whenever one of the amateur riders who paid to ride a horse complained when the horse wouldn't go. Mr. Evans would point to Lucy and say, "I bet this skinny little girl could get this horse to go." Lucy would climb into the saddle and because she knew how to ride, unlike the amateur paying customers, she would get the horse to fly.[243]

• Many Jewish sages have had "real" jobs. Rabbi Hillel was a woodcutter, Rabbi Shammai was a builder, Rabbi Joshua was a blacksmith, and Rabbi Hanina was a shoemaker. They understood the importance of work. One day some Rabbis were discussing the creation of the world, and they decided to ask Rabbi Joseph about it, because he was a builder and so would understand such things. When they arrived where Rabbi Joseph was working, he was on a scaffold and declined to come down, saying, "I was hired by the day, and my time belongs to my employer."[244]

• Ballet stage managers sometimes have strange duties. While dancing in Jerome Robbins' *Tyl Eulenspiegal*, Tanaquil Le Clercq released a helium-filled balloon into the air. Unfortunately, during the rest of the concert, the balloon lost helium and eventually made an appearance in a *Pas de Trois*, thus forming the fourth member of a *quatre*. After that mishap, the stage manager was given the job of shooting the balloon with a BB gun after the curtain closed on *Tyl Eulenspiegal*.[245]

• A Hasidic Rabbi was walking alone when he met a man. The Rabbi asked the man, "Who do you work for?" The man replied, "I'm the night watchman, and I work for the village. Who do you work for?" The Rabbi replied, "Sometimes I'm not sure, but I will offer you a job at twice your present salary. Your job will be to walk with me and from time to time to ask me, 'Who do you work for?'"[246]

• Caspar Wistar, a Quaker, first earned his living hauling ashes in a wheelbarrow, but later he became a mayor. Some of his opponents tried to embarrass him by wheeling a wheelbarrow outside his house, but Mr.

Wistar came out of his house and offered to show them how to wheel the wheelbarrow correctly.[247]

Zen

• Zen master Kangan once pointed to some boats on the sea and said to his disciple Daichi, "You speak of mind over matter — let's see you stop those boats from sailing." Daichi quietly put a screen between them and the boats, shutting off the sight of the boats. Kangan smiled, but pointed out, "You had to use your hands." Daichi closed his eyes.[248]

• Sakyamuni asked his disciples, "How long is a person's life?" His disciples guessed various lengths, such as 70 years, 60 years, etc., but Sakyamuni rejected all these answers. After his disciples gave up guessing, Sakyamuni answered his own question, "Life is but a breath."[249]

• A famous Zen master from Korea came to the United States. When he was asked where he wanted to go, he replied, "Las Vegas." This sounds shocking, but be assured that the Zen master didn't gamble. He had heard from other Koreans about the bright lights at Las Vegas, and he wanted to see the bright lights for himself.[250]

Appendix A: Book Bibliography

Alda, Frances. *Men, Women, and Tenors*. Boston, MA: Houghton Mifflin Company, 1937.

Aldrich, Jr., Nelson W., editor. *George Being George*. New York: Random House, 2008.

Ashley, Merrill. *Dancing for Balanchine*. New York: E.P. Dutton, Inc., 1984.

Aucoin, Kevyn. Face*Forward*. Boston, MA: Little, Brown and Company, 2000.

Aucoin, Kevyn. *Making Faces*. New York: Little, Brown and Company, 1997.

Ayre, Leslie. *The Wit of Music*. Boston, MA: Crescendo Publishing Company, 1969.

Barber, David W. *Bach, Beethoven, and the Boys*. Toronto, Canada: Sound and Vision, 1996.

Birin, Eileen, compiler and editor. *Chalkboard Dust: Twenty-six True Stories About Students as Remembered by Their Teachers*. Glendale, AR: Neelie Publishing, 1996.

Bock, Jannika. *Riot Grrrl: A Feminist Re-Interpretation of the Punk Narrative*. Saarbrücke: VDM Verlag Dr. Müller, 2008.

Borge, Victor, and Robert Sherman. *My Favorite Comedies in Music*. New York: Franklin Watts, 1980.

Borge, Victor, and Robert Sherman. *My Favorite Intermissions*. Garden City, NY: Doubleday and Co., Inc., 1971.

Boyden, John, collector. *Stick to the Music: Scores of Orchestral Tales*. London: Souvenir Press, 1992.

Bracken, Peg. *On Getting Old for the First Time*. Wilsonville, OR: BookPartners, Inc., 1997.

Bracken, Peg. *A Window Over the Sink*. New York: Harcourt Brace Jovanovich, Inc., 1981.

Callas, Evangelia. *My Daughter Maria Callas*. New York: Fleet Publishing Corporation, 1960.

Cardus, Neville, editor. *Kathleen Ferrier: A Memoir*. London: Hamish Hamilton, Ltd., 1954.

Carle, Eric. *Flora and Tiger: 19 Very Short Stories from My Life*. New York: Philomel Books, 1997.

Carson, Mina, Tisa Lewis, and Susan M. Shaw. *Girls Rock! Fifty Years of Women Making Music*. Lexington, KY: University Press of Kentucky, 2004.

Caruso, Dorothy. *Enrico Caruso: His Life and Death*. New York: Simon and Schuster, Inc., 1945.

Chan, Luke. *101 Lessons of Tao*. Cincinnati, OH: Benefactor Books, 1995.

Charles, Helen White, collector and editor. *Quaker Chuckles and Other True Stories About Friends*. Oxford, OH: H.W. Charles, 1961.

Chotzinoff, Samuel. *Toscanini: An Intimate Portrait*. New York: Alfred A. Knopf, 1956.

Clercq, Tanaquil Le. *The Ballet Cook Book*. New York: Stein and Day, Publishers, 1966.

Cott, Ted. *The Victor Book of Musical Fun*. New York: Simon and Schuster, Inc., 1945.

Cruz, Bárbara C. *José Clemente Orozco: Mexican Artist*. Berkeley Heights, NJ: Enslow Publications, Inc., 1998.

Czerny, Carl. *On the Proper Performance of All Beethoven's Piano Works*. Edited by Paul Badura-Skoda. USA: Universal Edition, 1970.

Deedy, John. *A Book of Catholic Anecdotes*. Allen, TX: Thomas More, 1997.

Diamond, Kerry. *Kevyn Aucoin: A Beautiful Life*. New York: Atria Books, 2003.

Domingo, Plácido. *My First Forty Years*. New York: Alfred A Knopf, 1983.

Douglas, Nigel. *More Legendary Voices*. London: Andre Deutsch Limited, 1994.

Eichenbaum, Rose. *Masters of Movement: Portraits of America's Great Choreographers*. Washington, DC: Smithsonian Books, 2004.

Eisenberg, Barbara. *Conversations with Frank Gehry*. New York: Alfred A. Knopf, 2009.

Erskine, Carl. *Carl Erskine's Tales from the Dodger Dugout*. Champaigne, IL: Sports Publishing Inc., 2000.

Ewen, David. *Dictators of the Baton*. Chicago, IL: Ziff-Davis Publishing Company, 1948.

Ewen, David. *Famous Modern Conductors*. New York: Dodd, Mead & Company, 1967.

Fadiman, James and Robert Frager. *Essential Sufism*. San Francisco, CA: HarperSanFrancisco, 1997.

Finck, Henry T. *Musical Laughs*. New York: Funk & Wagnalls Company, 1924.

Garden, Mary, and Louis Biancolli. *Mary Garden's Story*. New York: Simon and Schuster, Inc., 1951.

Geier, Arnold. *Heroes of the Holocaust*. Miami, FL: Londonbooks, 1993.

Goldstein, Ernest. *The Journey of Diego Rivera*. Minneapolis, MN: Lerner Publications Company, 1996.

Goodman, Philip. *Rejoice in Thy Festival*. New York: Bloch Publishing Company, 1956.

Groover, David L., and Cecil C. Conner, Jr. *Skeletons from the Opera Closet*. New York: St. Martin's Press, 1986.

Hewlett-Davies, Barry, editor and compiler. *A Night at the Opera*. New York: St. Martin's Press, 1980.

Heylbut, Rose, and Aimé Gerber. *Backstage at the Opera*. New York: Thomas Y. Crowell Company, 1937.

Himelstein, Shmuel. *A Touch of Wisdom, A Touch of Wit*. Brooklyn, NY: Mesorah Publications, Limited, 1991.

Himelstein, Shmuel. *Words of Wisdom, Words of Wit*. Brooklyn, NY: Mesorah Publications, Ltd., 1993.

Hinton, Milt, David G. Berger, and Holly Maxson. *Playing the Changes: Milt Hinton's Life in Stories and Photographs*. Nashville, TN: Vanderbilt University Press, 2008.

Hoff, Benjamin. *The Way to Life: At the Heart of the* Tao Te Ching. New York: Weatherhill, 1981.

Holloway, Gary. *Saints, Demons, and Asses: Southern Preacher Anecdotes*. Bloomington, IN: Indiana University Press, 1989.

Humphrey, Laning, compiler. *The Humor of Music and Other Oddities in the Art*. Boston, MA: Crescendo Publishing Company, 1971.

Jacobs, J. Vernon, compiler. *450 True Stories from Church History*. Grand Rapids, MI: Wm. B. Eerdmans Publishing Company, 1955.

Jesella, Kara, and Marisa Melitzer. *How SASSY Changed My Life: A Love Letter to the Greatest Teen Magazine of All Time*. New York: Faber and Faber, Inc., 2007.

Jampol, Joshua. *Living Opera*. Oxford: Oxford University Press, 2010.

Juno, Andrea, and V. Vale, editors. *Angry Women*. San Francisco, CA: Re/Search Publications, 1999.

Juno, Andrea, and V. Vale, publishers and editors. *Pranks! Devious Deeds and Mischievous Mirth*. San Francisco, CA: Re/Search Publications, 1987.

Kaufmann, Helen L. *Anecdotes of Music and Musicians*. New York: Grosset & Dunlap, Publishers, 1960.

Kenefick, Colleen, and Amy Y. Young, compilers and editors. *The Best of Nursing Humor*. Philadelphia, PA: Hanley & Belfus, Inc., 1993.

King-Smith, Dick. *Chewing the Cud*. New York: Alfred A. Knopf, 2001.

Klinger, Kurt, collector. *A Pope Laughs: Stories of John XXIII*. Translated by Sally McDevitt Cunneen. New York: Holt, Rinehart and Winston, 1964.

Kornfield, Jack, and Christina Feldman. *Soul Food: Stories to Nourish the Spirit and the Heart*. San Francisco, CA: HarperSanFrancisco, 1996. This is a revised edition of their 1991 book *Stories of the Spirit, Stories of the Heart*.

Lahee, Henry C. *Famous Singers of To-day and Yesterday*. Boston: L.C. Page and Company, 1898.

Lawrence, Marjorie. *Interrupted Melody: The Story of My Life*. New York: Appleton-Century-Crofts, Inc., 1949.

Lehmann, Lotte. *Midway in My Song: The Autobiography of Lotte Lehmann*. Freeport, NY: Books for Libraries Press, 1970.

Levant, Oscar. *A Smattering of Ignorance*. New York: Doubleday, Doran, and Co., 1940.

Lewis, Barbara A. *Kids with Courage: Stories About Young People Making a Difference*. Minneapolis, MN: Free Spirit Publishing, Inc., 1992.

Linkletter, Art. *Women are My Favorite People*. Garden City, NY: Doubleday & Company, Inc., 1974.

Mandelbaum, Yitta Halberstam. *Holy Brother: Inspiring Stories and Enchanted Tales About Rabbi Shlomo Carlebach*. Northvale, NJ: Jason Aronson, Inc., 1997.

Mapleson, Colonel J.H. *The Mapleson Memoirs: The Career of an Operatic Impresario, 1858-1888*. Edited by Harold Rosenthal. New York: Appleton-Century, 1966.

Marberry, Craig. *Cuttin' Up: Wit and Wisdom from Black Barber Shops*. New York: Doubleday, 2005.

Marcus, Leonard S., compiler and editor. *Funny Business: Conversations with Writers of Comedy*. Somerset, MA: Candlewick Press, 2009.

Marcus, Leonard S. *Ways of Telling: Conversations on the Art of the Picture Book*. New York: Dutton Children's Books, 2002.

Matthews, Denis. *In Pursuit of Music*. London: Victor Gollancz, Ltd., 1966.

Meek, Harold. *Horn and Conductor: Reminiscences of a Practitioner with a Few Words of Advice*. Rochester, NY: University of Rochester Press, 1997.

Mendelsohn, S. Felix. *Here's a Good One: Stories of Jewish Wit and Wisdom*. New York: Block Publishing Co., 1947.

Michaels, Louis. *The Humor and Warmth of Pope John XXIII: His Anecdotes and Legends*. New York: Pocket Books, Inc., 1965.

Molen, Sam. *Take 2 and Hit to Right*. Philadelphia, PA: Dorrance and Company, 1959.

Moore, Dudley. *Musical Bumps*. London: Robson Books, 1986.

Muallimoglu, Nejat. *The Wit and Wisdom of Nasraddin Hodja*. New York: Cynthia Parzych Publishing, Inc., 1986.

Nachman, Gerald. *Seriously Funny: The Rebel Comedians of the 1950s and 1960s*. New York: Pantheon Books, 2003.

Nash, Bruce, and Allan Zullo. *The Greatest Sports Stories Never Told*. Compiled by Bernie Ward. New York: Simon and Schuster Books for Young Readers, 1993.

Peck, Donald. *The Right Time, The Right Place! Tales of Chicago Symphony Days*. Bloomington and Indianapolis, IN: Indiana University Press, 2007.

Penzler, Otto, editor. *The Lineup*. New York: Little, Brown and Company, 2009.

Poley, Irvin C., and Ruth Verlenden Poley. *Friendly Anecdotes*. New York: Harper & Brothers, Publishers, 1950.

Porter, Alyene. *Papa was a Preacher*. New York: Abingdon Press, 1944.

Rabinowicz, Rabbi Dr. H. *A Guide to Hassidism*. New York: Thomas Yoseloff, 1960.

Rayfield, Susan. *Pierre-Auguste Renoir*. New York: Harry N. Abrams, Publishers, 1998.

Reisfeld, Randi, and Marie Morreale. *Got Issues Much: Celebrities Share Their Traumas and Triumphs*. New York: Scholastic Inc., 1999.

Ringwald, Molly. *Getting the Pretty Back: Friendship, Family, and Finding the Perfect Lipstick*. New York: HarperCollins Publishers, 2010.

Roessel, Monty. *Songs from the Loom: A Navajo Girl Learns to Weave*. Minneapolis, MN: Lerner Publications Company, 1995.

Rollins, Henry. *Get in the Van: On the Road with Black Flag*. Los Angeles, CA: 2.13.61, 2004.

Rosen, Michael J., editor. *Horse People: Writers and Artists on the Horses They Love*. New York: Workman Publishing Company, Inc., 1998.

Rowell, Edward K., editor. *Humor for Preaching and Teaching*. Grand Rapids, MI: Baker Books, 1996.

Salkin, Jeffrey K. *Being God's Partner: How to Find the Hidden Link Between Spirituality and Your Work*. Woodstock, VT: Jewish Lights Publishing, 1994.

Salzberg, Sharon. *A Heart as Wide as the World: Stories on the Path to Lovingkindness*. Boston, MA: Shambhala Publications, Inc., 1997.

Salzberg, Sharon. *Lovingkindness: The Revolutionary Art of Happiness*. Boston, MA: Shambhala Publications, Inc., 1995.

Samra, Cal and Rose, editors. *Holy Hilarity*. Colorado Springs, CO: WaterBrook Press, 1999.

Scieszka, Jon. *Knucklehead: Tall Tales and Mostly True Stories About Growing Up Scieszka*. New York: Viking, 2008.

Sessions, William H., collector. *Laughter in Quaker Grey*. York, England: William Sessions, Limited, 1966.

Sessions, William H., collector. *More Quaker Laughter*. York, England: William Sessions, Limited, 1974.

Sheridan, Martin. *Comics and Their Creators: Life Stories of American Cartoonists*. Westport, CT: Hyperion Press, Inc., 1977.

Shydner, Ritch, and Mark Schiff, compilers. *I Killed: True Stories of the Road from America's Top Comics*. New York: Crown Publishers, 2006.

Silverman, William B. *Rabbinic Wisdom and Jewish Values*. New York: Union of American Hebrew Congregations, 1971.

Smoot, Bill. *Conversations with Great Teachers*. Bloomington, IN: Indiana University Press, 2010.

Soyer, Raphael. *A Painter's Pilgrimage: An Account of a Journey with Drawings by the Author*. New York: Crown Publishers, Inc., 1962.

Stryk, Lucien, and Takashi Ikemoto, selectors and translators. *Zen: Poems, Prayers, Sermons, Anecdotes, Interviews*. Chicago, IL: Swallow Press, 1981.

Telushkin, Rabbi Joseph. *Jewish Humor: What the Best Jewish Jokes Say About the Jews*. New York: William Morrow and Company, 1992.

Telushkin, Rabbi Joseph. *Jewish Wisdom: Ethical, Spiritual, and Historical Lessons from the Great Works and Thinkers*. New York: William Morrow and Company, Inc., 1994.

Thomas, Marlo. *Growing Up Laughing: My Story and the Story of Funny*. Waterville, ME: Thorndike Press, 2010. Large Print.

Tsai, Chih-Chung. *Zen Speaks: Shouts of Nothingness*. New York: Anchor Books, 1994.

Voss, Frederick S. *Women of Our Time: An Album of Twentieth-Century Portraits*. London: Merrell in association with the National Portrait Gallery, Smithsonian Institution, 2002.

Wells, Steven. *Punk: Young, Loud, and Snotty*. New York: Thunder's Mouth Press, 2004.

Wiesel, Elie. *Souls on Fire: Portraits and Legends of Hasidic Masters*. Translated from the French by Marion Wiesel. New York: Random House, 1972.

Williams, Heidi, editor. *Body Image*. Detroit, MI: Greenhaven Press, 2009.

Woollcott, Barbara. *None But a Mule*. New York: The Viking Press, 1944.

Appendix B: About the Author

It was a dark and stormy night. Suddenly a cry rang out, and on a hot summer night in 1954, Josephine, wife of Carl Bruce, gave birth to a boy — me. Unfortunately, this young married couple allowed Reuben Saturday, Josephine's brother, to name their first-born. Reuben, aka "The Joker," decided that Bruce was a nice name, so he decided to name me Bruce Bruce. I have gone by my middle name — David — ever since.

Being named Bruce David Bruce hasn't been all bad. Bank tellers remember me very quickly, so I don't often have to show an ID. It can be fun in charades, also. When I was a counselor as a teenager at Camp Echoing Hills in Warsaw, Ohio, a fellow counselor gave the signs for "sounds like" and "two words," then she pointed to a bruise on her leg twice. Bruise Bruise? Oh yeah, Bruce Bruce is the answer!

Uncle Reuben, by the way, gave me a haircut when I was in kindergarten. He cut my hair short and shaved a small bald spot on the back of my head. My mother wouldn't let me go to school until the bald spot grew out again.

Of all my brothers and sisters (six in all), I am the only transplant to Athens, Ohio. I was born in Newark, Ohio, and have lived all around Southeastern Ohio. However, I moved to Athens to go to Ohio University and have never left.

At Ohio U, I never could make up my mind whether to major in English or Philosophy, so I got a bachelor's degree with a double major in both areas, then I added a Master of Arts degree in English and a Master of Arts degree in Philosophy. Yes, I have my MAMA degree.

Currently, and for a long time to come (I eat fruits and veggies), I am spending my retirement writing books such as *Nadia Comaneci: Perfect 10*, *The Funniest People in Comedy*, *Homer's* Iliad: *A Retelling in Prose*, and *William Shakespeare's* Hamlet: *A Retelling in Prose.*

If all goes well, I will publish one or two books a year for the rest of my life. (On the other hand, a good way to make God laugh is to tell Her your plans.)

By the way, my sister Brenda Kennedy writes romances such as *A New Beginning* and *Shattered Dreams.*

Appendix C: Some Books by David Bruce

Anecdote Collections

250 Anecdotes About Opera
250 Anecdotes About Religion
250 Anecdotes About Religion: Volume 2
250 Music Anecdotes
Be a Work of Art: 250 Anecdotes and Stories
Boredom is Anti-Life: 250 Anecdotes and Stories
The Coolest People in Art: 250 Anecdotes
The Coolest People in the Arts: 250 Anecdotes
The Coolest People in Books: 250 Anecdotes
The Coolest People in Comedy: 250 Anecdotes
Create, Then Take a Break: 250 Anecdotes
Don't Fear the Reaper: 250 Anecdotes
The Funniest People in Art: 250 Anecdotes
The Funniest People in Books: 250 Anecdotes
The Funniest People in Books, Volume 2: 250 Anecdotes
The Funniest People in Books, Volume 3: 250 Anecdotes
The Funniest People in Comedy: 250 Anecdotes
The Funniest People in Dance: 250 Anecdotes
The Funniest People in Families: 250 Anecdotes
The Funniest People in Families, Volume 2: 250 Anecdotes
The Funniest People in Families, Volume 3: 250 Anecdotes
The Funniest People in Families, Volume 4: 250 Anecdotes
The Funniest People in Families, Volume 5: 250 Anecdotes
The Funniest People in Families, Volume 6: 250 Anecdotes
The Funniest People in Movies: 250 Anecdotes
The Funniest People in Music: 250 Anecdotes
The Funniest People in Music, Volume 2: 250 Anecdotes
The Funniest People in Music, Volume 3: 250 Anecdotes
The Funniest People in Neighborhoods: 250 Anecdotes
The Funniest People in Relationships: 250 Anecdotes
The Funniest People in Sports: 250 Anecdotes
The Funniest People in Sports, Volume 2: 250 Anecdotes
The Funniest People in Television and Radio: 250 Anecdotes

The Funniest People in Theater: 250 Anecdotes
The Funniest People Who Live Life: 250 Anecdotes
The Funniest People Who Live Life, Volume 2: 250 Anecdotes
The Kindest People Who Do Good Deeds, Volume 1: 250 Anecdotes
The Kindest People Who Do Good Deeds, Volume 2: 250 Anecdotes
Maximum Cool: 250 Anecdotes
The Most Interesting People in Movies: 250 Anecdotes
The Most Interesting People in Politics and History: 250 Anecdotes
The Most Interesting People in Politics and History, Volume 2: 250 Anecdotes
The Most Interesting People in Politics and History, Volume 3: 250 Anecdotes
The Most Interesting People in Religion: 250 Anecdotes
The Most Interesting People in Sports: 250 Anecdotes
The Most Interesting People Who Live Life: 250 Anecdotes
The Most Interesting People Who Live Life, Volume 2: 250 Anecdotes
Reality is Fabulous: 250 Anecdotes and Stories
Resist Psychic Death: 250 Anecdotes
Seize the Day: 250 Anecdotes and Stories

[1]Source: Jannika Bock, *Riot Grrrl: A Feminist Re-Interpretation of the Punk Narrative*, p. 75. Also: Bárbara C. Cruz, *José Clemente Orozco: Mexican Artist*, p. 101.

[2] Source: Oliver Burkeman, "Politeness enforcement tactics." *The Guardian*. 28 August 2010 <http://www.guardian.co.uk/lifeandstyle/2010/aug/28/change-your-life-politeness-enforcement>.

[3] Source: Jonathan Jones, "Student protests: the riot girls." *The Guardian*. 25 November 2010 <http://www.guardian.co.uk/uk/2010/nov/25/student-protests-tuition-fees-schoolgirls-definace>. Also: <en.wiktionary.org/wiki/kettling>, accessed on 26 November 2010.

[4] Source: Steven Wells, *Punk: Young, Loud, and Snotty*, pp. 68, 78.

[5] Source: Andrea Juno and V. Vale, publishers and editors, *Pranks! Devious Deeds and Mischievous Mirth*, p. 134.

[6]Source: J. Vernon Jacobs, compiler, *450 True Stories from Church History*, p. 70.

[7] Source: Frederick S. Voss, *Women of Our Time: An Album of Twentieth-Century Portraits*, pp. 28-29.

[8]Source: John Deedy, *A Book of Catholic Anecdotes*, pp. 43-44.

[9] Source: Andrea Juno and V. Vale, publishers and editors, *Pranks! Devious Deeds and Mischievous Mirth*, p. 135.

[10] Source: Leonard S. Marcus, *Ways of Telling: Conversations on the Art of the Picture Book*, pp. 44-47.

[11] Source: Kara Jesella and Marisa Melitzer, *How SASSY Changed My Life: A Love Letter to the Greatest Teen Magazine of All Time*, p. 51.

[12] Source: Arnold Geier, *Heroes of the Holocaust*, pp. 39-43.

[13] Source: Eric Carle, *Flora and Tiger: 19 Very Short Stories from My Life*, pp. 52-54.

[14]Source: Dorothy Caruso, *Enrico Caruso: His Life and Death*, pp. 35-36.

[15] Source: Michael J. Rosen, editor, *Horse People: Writers and Artists on the Horses They Love*, pp. 61-63.

[16] Source: Raphael Soyer, *A Painter's Pilgrimage: An Account of a Journey with Drawings by the Author*, p. 58.

[17]Source: Louis Michaels, *The Humor and Warmth of Pope John XXIII*, p. 15.

[18] Source: Rose Eichenbaum, *Masters of Movement: Portraits of America's Great Choreographers*, p. 94.

[19] Source: Merrill Ashley, *Dancing for Balanchine*, p. 2.

[20] Source: Otto Penzler, editor, *The Lineup*, pp. 351-353.

[21] Source: Leonard S. Marcus, compiler and editor, *Funny Business: Conversations with Writers of Comedy*, pp. 5-6.

[22] Source: Kerry Diamond, *Kevyn Aucoin: A Beautiful Life*, p. 124.

[23] Source: Monica Buchanan, "Snowplow leads way to hospital for expectant mom." NBCNewYork.com. 30 January 2011 <http://www.msnbc.msn.com/id/41339306/ns/us_news-wonderful_world/>.

[24] Source: Marlo Thomas, *Growing Up Laughing: My Story and the Story of Funny*, pp. 76-79.

[25] Source: Craig Marberry, *Cuttin' Up: Wit and Wisdom from Black Barber Shops*, pp. 70, 74.

[26] Source: Barbara Woollcott, *None But a Mule*, pp. 71-72.

[27] Source: Molly Ringwald, *Getting the Pretty Back: Friendship, Family, and Finding the Perfect Lipstick*, pp. 216, 228.

[28] Source: Art Linkletter, *Women are My Favorite People*, p. 126.

[29] Source: Raphael Soyer, *A Painter's Pilgrimage: An Account of a Journey with Drawings by the Author*, pp. 71-72.

[30] Source: Colin Robinson, "The Trouble With Amazon." *The Nation*. 14 July 2010 <http://www.thenation.com/article/37484/trouble-amazon>. Note: This article also appeared in the August 2/9, 2010 edition of *The Nation*.

[31] Source: Edward Rothstein, "Monkey Business in a World of Evil." *The New York Times*. 25 March 2010 <http://www.nytimes.com/2010/03/26/arts/design/26curious.html?pagewanted=all>.

[32] Source: David Ewen, *Famous Modern Conductors*, p. 142.

[33] Source: William H. Sessions, collector, *More Quaker Laughter*, p. 94.

[34] Source: Tom Matlack, "Memories of Dad at Christmas." Huffington Post. 25 December 2010 <http://www.huffingtonpost.com/tom-matlack/memories-of-dad-at-christ_b_800643.html>.

[35] Source: K. Lynn Wieck, *Stories for Nurses: Acts of Caring*, pp. 63-64.

[36] Source: Omar Villafranca, "The Santa Who Speaks With His Hands." Nbcdfw.com. 23 December 2010 <http://www.nbcdfw.com/news/local-beat/The-Santa-that-Speaks-with-his-Hands-112365444.html>.

[37] Source: Alyene Porter, *Papa was a Preacher*, pp. 135-136.

[38] Source: Cal and Rose Samra, *Holy Hilarity*, pp. 178-179.

[39] Source: Edward K. Rowell, editor, *Humor for Preaching and Teaching*, p. 165.

[40] Source: Gary Holloway, *Saints, Demons, and Asses*, p. 66.

[41] Source: "Mary J Blige gives stranger designer togs." *Stuff* (New Zealand). 19 June 2008 <http://www.stuff.co.nz/life-style/fashion/495677>.

[42] Source: Mary Garden and Louis Biancolli, *Mary Garden's Story*, pp. 181-182.

[43] Source: Henry Rollins, *Get in the Van: On the Road with Black Flag*, p. 37.

[44] Source: William B. Silverman, *Rabbinic Wisdom and Jewish Values*, p. 42.

[45] Source: Tanaquil Le Clercq, *The Ballet Cook Book*, p. 353.

[46] Source: David Martindale, "Cheech & Chong still rolling out 'stoner' routines for big laughs." McClatchy Newspapers. 28 April 2010 <http://www.popmatters.com/pm/article/124728-cheech-chong-still-rolling-out-stoner-routines-for-big-laughs/>.

[47] Source: Ritch Shydner and Mark Schiff, compilers, *I Killed: True Stories of the Road from America's Top Comics*, p. 195.

[48] Source: Gerald Nachman, *Seriously Funny*, p. 601.

[49] Source: Lotte Lehmann, *Midway in My Song*, pp. 226-227.

[50] Source: Oscar Levant, *A Smattering of Ignorance*, pp. 34-35.

[51] Source: Dudley Moore, *Musical Bumps*, p. 82.

[52] Source: Harold Meek, *Horn and Conductor*, p. 24.

[53] Source: David Ewen, *Dictators of the Baton*, p. 46.

[54] Source: Randi Reisfeld and Marie Morreale, *Got Issues Much: Celebrities Share Their Traumas and Triumphs*, pp. 93-94.

[55] Source: Ritch Shydner and Mark Schiff, compilers, *I Killed: True Stories of the Road from America's Top Comics*, p. 93.

[56] Source: Craig Marberry, *Cuttin' Up: Wit and Wisdom from Black Barber Shops*, pp. 22-24.

[57] Source: Frederick S. Voss, *Women of Our Time: An Album of Twentieth-Century Portraits*, pp. 106-107.

[58] Source: Elie Wiesel, *Souls on Fire*, p. 49.

[59] Source: Rabbi Dr. H. Rabinowicz, *A Guide to Hassidism*, p. 39.

[60] Source: Chih Chung Tsai, *Zen Speaks*, p. 63.

[61] Source: Barry Hewlett-Davies, *A Night at the Opera*, p. 75.

[62] Source: David L. Groover and Cecil C. Conner, Jr., *Skeletons from the Opera Closet*, p. 42.

[63] Source: Dudley Moore, *Musical Bumps*, p. 162.

[64] Source: Ted Cott, *The Victor Book of Musical Fun*, p. 23.

[65] Source: Rabbi Joseph Telushkin, *Jewish Wisdom*, p. 13.

[66] Source: Rabbi Joseph Telushkin, *Jewish Wisdom*, pp. 62-63.

[67] Source: William B. Silverman, *Rabbinic Wisdom and Jewish Values*, pp. 162-163.

[68] Source: Henry C. Lahee, *Famous Singers of To-day and Yesterday*, p. 100.

[69] Source: Nejat Muallimoglu, *The Wit and Wisdom of Nasraddin Hodja*, p. 139.

[70] Source: Milt Hinton, David G. Berger, and Holly Maxson, *Playing the Changes: Milt Hinton's Life in Stories and Photographs*, pp. 74, 107, 111.

[71] Source: Colleen Kenefick and Amy Y. Young, compilers and editors, *The Best of Nursing Humor*, pp. 28-30.

[72] Source: Roger Ebert, "Ten things I know about the mosque." *Roger Ebert's Journal.* 14 December 2012 < **https://www.rogerebert.com/roger-ebert/ten-things-i-know-about-the-mosque** >.

[73] Source: Barbara Woollcott, *None But a Mule*, pp. 27-28, 140-141.

[74] Source: Bill Smoot, *Conversations with Great Teachers*, pp. 127, 129.

[75] Source: Eileen Birin, compiler and editor, *Chalkboard Dust*, pp. 188-195.

[76] Source: Sharon Salzberg, *Lovingkindness*, p. 141.

[77] Source: Heidi Williams, editor. *Body Image*, pp. 49, 54.

[78] Source: Rabbi Joseph Telushkin, *Jewish Humor*, p. 55.

[79] Source: Molly Ringwald, *Getting the Pretty Back: Friendship, Family, and Finding the Perfect Lipstick*, p. 220.

[80] Source: Sharon Salzberg, *Lovingkindness*, pp. 39-40.

[81] Source: Joshua Jampol, *Living Opera*, pp. 317-318.

[82] Source: Monty Roessel, *Songs from the Loom: A Navajo Girl Learns to Weave*, pp. 11, 34, 46.

[83] Source: Nelson W. Aldrich, Jr., editor, *George Being George*, pp. 63, 81.

[84] Source: Steve Lopez, "1,100 students later ... some thoughts on teaching." *Los Angeles Times*. 9 June 2010 <http://www.latimes.com/news/local/orange/la-me-lopezcolumn-20100609,0,5929433.column>.

[85] Source: Barbara Eisenberg, *Conversations with Frank Gehry*, pp. 184-185.

[86] Source: Mina Carson, Tisa Lewis, and Susan M. Shaw, *Girls Rock! Fifty Years of Women Making Music*, p. 7.

[87] Source: Sharon Salzberg, *A Heart as Wide as the World*, pp. 7-8.

[88] Source: Henry T. Finck, *Musical Laughs*, pp. 238-239.

[89] Source: Lucien Stryk and Takashi Ikemoto, selectors and translators, *Zen: Poems, Prayers, Sermons, Anecdotes, Interviews*, p. xli.

[90] Source: Elie Wiesel, *Souls on Fire*, p. 154.

[91] Source: S. Felix Mendelsohn, *Here's a Good One*, p. 163.

[92] Source: Kevyn Aucoin, Face*Forward*, pp. 28-29, 40-43, 46-47, 64-67, 104-105, 112-113.

[93] Source: Leslie Ayre, *The Wit of Music*, p. 58.

[94] Source: Lotte Lehmann, *Midway in My Song*, pp. 239-240.

[95] Source: Otto Penzler, editor, *The Lineup*, pp. 202, 208-209.

[96] Source: Victor Borge and Robert Sherman, *My Favorite Comedies in Music*, p. 100.

[97] Source: Filed by Erica Liepmann, "Daniel Chung: New Zealand Taxi Driver Feeds Homeless Each Week Out Of His Own Pocket." Huffington Post. 10 May 2010 <http://www.huffingtonpost.com/2010/05/10/daniel-chung-new-zealand_n_570457.html>. Also: Jo Mckenzie-Mclean, "One man's heartfelt handout." *The Press* (New Zealand). 5 October 2010 <http://www.stuff.co.nz/the-press/news/3674385/One-mans-heartfelt-handout>.

[98] Source: Helen White Charles, collector and editor, *Quaker Chuckles*, p. 35.

[99] Source: Peg Bracken, *On Getting Old for the First Time*, pp. 30, 81.

[100] Source: Rose Heylbut and Aimé Gerber, *Backstage at the Opera*, p. 136.

[101] Source: Randi Reisfeld and Marie Morreale, *Got Issues Much: Celebrities Share Their Traumas and Triumphs*, pp. 197-200.

[102] Source: Samuel Chotzinoff, *Toscanini: An Intimate Portrait*, pp. 48-52.

[103] Source: Nigel Douglas, *More Legendary Voices*, p. 220.

[104] Source: Laning Humphrey, compiler, *The Humor of Music and Other Oddities in the Art*, p. 62.

[105] Source: Oneluckylady, "A Circle of Kindness Started by a 10 Year Old Girl." Dailygood.org. <http://www.dailygood.org/view.php?qid=4394>. Accessed on 7 February 2011. This is one of the "Top 10 Kindness Stories of 2010."

[106] Source: Kerry Diamond, *Kevyn Aucoin: A Beautiful Life*, pp. 28-29, 84, 119, 132-133, 203.

[107] Source: Kathryn Hawkins, "Reddit Online Community Helps Family Bring Long-Lost Music to Life." Gimundo.com. 14 April 2010 < https://tinyurl.com/2k5fzmbk >.

[108] Henry Rollins, "LA WEEKLY COLUMN #17." *LA Weekly*. 12 December 2010 <http://henryrollins.com/news/detail/la_weekly_column_17/>.

[109] Source: Arnold Geier, *Heroes of the Holocaust*, pp. 246-250.

[110] Source: Barbara A. Lewis, *Kids with Courage: Stories About Young People Making a Difference*, pp. 99-103.

[111] Source: "Violinist plays for taxi driver." BBC News. 7 May 2008 <http://news.bbc.co.uk/2/hi/7385174.stm>. Also: "Honest Muslim Taxi Driver Returns $4,000,000 Violin." <http://www.youtube.com/watch?v=cGivELEG0Ko&feature=watch_response>. Also: "Mohammed Khalil (Newark Cabbie) Fan Club." Facebook. <http://www.facebook.com/group.php?gid=20099800615>. Accessed on 21 December 2010.

[112] Source: Kathryn Hawkins, "Bystander Angela Pierce Protects Police Officer from Suspect Attack." Gimundo.com. 17 December 2010 <http://tinyurl.com/yery49x8>. Also: Steve Bennish, "'Angel' recounts day she helped cop." *Dayton Daily News*. 18 December 2010 < http://tinyurl.com/cru7jk23 >.

[113] Source: Eva Orchard, "Letter to the Editor: Good Samaritan helped reader after car stalled." *Standard-Examiner* (Utah). 12 January 2011 <http://www.standard.net/topics/opinion/2011/01/12/good-samaritan-helped-reader-after-car-stalled>.

[114] Source: "Honest Cabbie Rewarded." *The Nation* (Thailand). 28 September 2010 <http://www.nationmultimedia.com/home/2010/09/28/national/Honest-cabbie-rewarded-30138862.html>.

[115] Source: Yitta Halberstam Mandelbaum, *Holy Brother*, pp. 131-133.

[116] Source: Leonard S. Marcus, compiler and editor, *Funny Business: Conversations with Writers of Comedy*, p. 20.

[117] Source: Dorothy Caruso, *Enrico Caruso: His Life and Death*, p. 140.

[118] Source: Kurt Klinger, *A Pope Laughs*, p. 79.

[119] Source: Peg Bracken, *A Window Over the Sink*, pp. 138-139, 143-155.

[120] Source: Marlo Thomas, *Growing Up Laughing: My Story and the Story of Funny*, p. 158.

[121] Source: Jennifer Fermino, Erika Martinez and Peter Cox, "Jews' Subway Hero A Muslim: Saves 'Hanukkah' Riders From Thugs." *New York Post*. 12 December 2007 <http://www.nypost.com/p/news/regional/item_SF5elktAPxQgqd71DWLfyJ>. Also: "Hero Muslim saves Jew from Christian Thugs on NY Subway." CNN. <http://www.youtube.com/watch?v=Xlwc0mE0lCU>. Also: "ICNA Honors NY Subway Hero." Islamic Circle of North America. 1 January 2008 <http://www.icna.org/2008/01/>. Also: "Hassan Askari, Muslim Hero, attends Hanukkah Celebration." The Islamic Workplace. 15 December 2007 <http://makkah.wordpress.com/2007/12/15/hassan-askari-muslim-hero-attends-hanukkah-celebration/>.

[122] Source: Roia Delfiner, "12-year-old Long Island girl saves friend with move she learned from SpongeBob Square Pants." *New York Post*. 23 April 2010 <http://www.nypost.com/p/news/local/spongebob_hero_2BRjc83sAiydgatlOgmMYP#ixzz0lxBhvtD5>. Also: Frank Eltman, "Girl Helps Choking Friend, Credits 'SpongeBob.'" *Huffington Post*. 23 April 2010 <http://www.huffingtonpost.com/2010/04/23/spongebob-squarepants-to_n_549315.html>.

[123] Source: "Waleed Shaalan." <http://topics.nytimes.com/topics/reference/timestopics/people/s/waleed_shaalan/index.html>. Accessed 22 December 2010. Also: "Waleed Mohamed Shaalan." <http://www.vt-memorial.org/profiles/Shaalan.html>. Also: "Heroic Victim Distracted Crazed Gunman." Sky News. 20 April 2007 <http://news.sky.com/skynews/Home/Sky-News-Archive/Article/20080641261696>. Also: "Muslim Virginia Tech Student Gave His Life To Save Others." 26 April 2007 <https://theislamicworkplace.com/2007/04/26/muslim-va-student-gave-his-life-to-save-others/>. Also: "Muslim Virginia Tech Student Gave His Life To Save Others." 26 April 2007 <https://theislamicworkplace.com/2007/04/26/muslim-va-student-gave-his-life-to-save-others/>.

[124] Source: Neal Shusterman, *Kid Heroes: True Stories of Rescuers, Survivors, and Achievers*, pp. 4-6. Also: Associated Press, "Girl, 6, Rescues Sister From Plane Wreckage." 17 August 1986 <http://articles.latimes.com/1986-08-17/news/mn-16563_1_park-wardens>.

[125] Source: Pete Donohue, Ben Chapman and Rich Schapiro. "Good Samaritan fights off lunatic and pulls off-duty MTA employee from F train tracks." *New York Daily News*. 6 February 2011 < https://tinyurl.com/3sy3fzer >.

[126] Source: Imaeyen Ibanga and Karen Compton, "Boy Safely Steers Out-of-Control School Bus." ABCNews.com. 9 April 2008 <http://abcnews.go.com/GMA/story?id=4618932&page=1>. Also: ABC Video. <http://abcnews.go.com/video/playerIndex?id=4617457>.

[127] Source: "The Art Of Fiction No. 189, Stephen King." Interviewed by Christopher Lehmann-Haupt and Nathaniel Rich. *Paris Review*. Fall 2006. No. 178. <http://www.theparisreview.org/interviews/5653/the-art-of-fiction-no-189-stephen-king>.

[128] Source: Victor Borge and Robert Sherman, *My Favorite Intermissions*, p. 161.

[129] Source: Art Linkletter, *Women are My Favorite People*, p. 127.

[130] Source: David W. Barber, *Bach, Beethoven, and the Boys*, p. 74.

[131] Source: Susan Rayfield, *Pierre-Auguste Renoir*, pp. 78, 81-82, 87.

[132] Source: Rabbi Joseph Telushkin, *Jewish Wisdom*, p. 133.

[133] Source: David Ewen, *Famous Modern Conductors*, pp. 125-126.

[134] Source: Nelson W. Aldrich, Jr., editor, *George Being George*, p. 73.

[135] Source: Helen L. Kaufmann, *Anecdotes of Music and Musicians*, pp. 70-71.

[136]Source: Denis Matthews, *In Pursuit of Music*, p. 79.

[137]Source: Mary Garden and Louis Biancolli, *Mary Garden's Story*, pp. 90-92.

[138] Source: Carl Erskine, *Carl Erskine's Tales from the Dodger Dugout*, pp. 72-73.

[139]Source: Plácido Domingo, *My First Forty Years*, p. 116.

[140] Source: Donald Peck, *The Right Time, The Right Place! Tales of Chicago Symphony Days*, p. 8.

[141] Source: Sam Molen, *Take 2 and Hit to Right*, pp. 9-10.

[142]Source: Carl Czerny, *On the Proper Performance of All Beethoven's Piano Works*, p. 7.

[143] Source: Kevyn Aucoin, *Making Faces*, pp. 19, 21, 27, 37, 43.

[144] Source: Leonard S. Marcus, *Ways of Telling: Conversations on the Art of the Picture Book*, pp. 90-91.

[145] Source: Rose Eichenbaum, *Masters of Movement: Portraits of America's Great Choreographers*, p. 178.

[146] Source: Colleen Kenefick and Amy Y. Young, compilers and editors, *The Best of Nursing Humor*, pp. 13-14.

[147] Source: Roger Ebert, "I met a character by Charles Dickens." Roger Ebert's Journal. 5 February 2010 <http://blogs.suntimes.com/ebert/2010/02/i_lived_in_dickens_london.html>.

[148] Source: Jon Scieszka, *Knucklehead: Tall Tales and Mostly True Stories About Growing Up Scieszka*, pp. 13, 16.

[149] Source: Merrill Ashley, *Dancing for Balanchine*, pp. 13.

[150]Source: John Deedy, *A Book of Catholic Anecdotes*, p. 136.

[151]Source: Gary Holloway, *Saints, Demons, and Asses*, p. 54.

[152] Source: Associated Press, "Kenya village gets clinic from brothers it helped." 7 July 2008 <http://www.msnbc.msn.com/id/25573377/>.

[153] Source: Milt Hinton, David G. Berger, and Holly Maxson, *Playing the Changes: Milt Hinton's Life in Stories and Photographs*, pp. 29-30.

[154] Source: "Finders not keepers." *Stuff* (New Zealand). 3 November 2008 <http://www.stuff.co.nz/auckland/local-news/western-leader/701648>.

[155]Source: Shmuel Himelstein, *Words of Wisdom, Words of Wit*, pp. 265-266.

[156] Source: Daniel Lovering, "Anonymous Thief Pays For Stolen Hammer." Reuters. 20 December 2010 < **https://www.reuters.com/article/us-crime-hammer-idUSTRE6BJ45I20101220/** >.

[157] Source: Jack Kornfield and Christina Feldman, *Soul Food*, pp. 238-239.

[158] Source: Kurt Klinger, *A Pope Laughs*, p. 154.

[159] Source: Nejat Muallimoglu, *The Wit and Wisdom of Nasraddin Hodja*, p. 39.

[160] Source: Laning Humphrey, compiler, *The Humor of Music and Other Oddities in the Art*, pp. 93-94.

[161] Source: Philip Goodman, *Rejoice in Thy Festival*, pp. 232-233.

[162] Source: James Fadiman and Robert Frager, *Essential Sufism*, pp. 68-69.

[163] Source: Sam Molen, *Take 2 and Hit to Right*, p. 12.

[164] Source: Andrea Juno and V. Vale, editors, *Angry Women*, p. 185.

[165] Source: David Ewen, *Dictators of the Baton*, p. 132.

[166] Source: Martin Sheridan, *Comics and Their Creators: Life Stories of American Cartoonists*, p. 136.

[167] Source: J. Vernon Jacobs, compiler, *450 True Stories from Church History*, p. 129.

[168] Source: Steven Wells, *Punk: Young, Loud, and Snotty*, p. 73.

[169] Source: Kara Jesella and Marisa Melitzer, *How SASSY Changed My Life: A Love Letter to the Greatest Teen Magazine of All Time*, pp. 74-75.

[170] Source: Henry Rollins, *Get in the Van: On the Road with Black Flag*, pp. 43, 46-48, 149, 247.

[171] Source: Frances Alda, *Men, Women, and Tenors*, p. 252.

[172] Source: Samuel Chotzinoff, *Toscanini: An Intimate Portrait*, pp. 77-78.

[173] Source: Carl Czerny, *On the Proper Performance of All Beethoven's Piano Works*, pp. 15.

[174] Source: Neville Cardus, editor, *Kathleen Ferrier: A Memoir*, p. 56.

[175] Source: Victor Borge and Robert Sherman, *My Favorite Intermissions*, pp. 44-45.

[176] Source: Oscar Levant, *A Smattering of Ignorance*, pp. 27-28.

[177] Source: John Boyden, collector, *Stick to the Music: Scores of Orchestral Tales*, pp. 80-81.

[178]Source: Rose Heylbut and Aimé Gerber, *Backstage at the Opera*, pp. 149-150.

[179]Source: Harold Meek, *Horn and Conductor*, p. 59.

[180]Source: Henry C. Lahee, *Famous Singers of To-day and Yesterday*, p. 31.

[181]Source: Denis Matthews, *In Pursuit of Music*, p. 69.

[182] Source: Donald Peck, *The Right Time, The Right Place! Tales of Chicago Symphony Days*, pp. 60-61.

[183]Source: Ted Cott, *The Victor Book of Musical Fun*, p. 72.

[184]Source: David W. Barber, *Bach, Beethoven, and the Boys*, p. 80.

[185] Source: Jon Scieszka, *Knucklehead: Tall Tales and Mostly True Stories About Growing Up Scieszka*, pp. 64-66.

[186] Source: Joshua Jampol, *Living Opera*, pp. 80, 82.

[187] Source: Peg Bracken, *On Getting Old for the First Time*, pp. 15, 28-29, 104.

[188]Source: Edward K. Rowell, editor, *Humor for Preaching and Teaching*, p. 152.

[189]Source: Plácido Domingo, *My First Forty Years*, p. 91.

[190] Source: Andrea Juno and V. Vale, editors, *Angry Women*, pp. 118, 120.

[191] Source: Dick King-Smith, *Chewing the Cud*, pp. 66-67.

[192] Source: Barbara A. Lewis, *Kids with Courage: Stories About Young People Making a Difference*, pp. 74-77.

[193] Source: Carl Erskine, *Carl Erskine's Tales from the Dodger Dugout*, p. 60.

[194] Source: Eric Carle, *Flora and Tiger: 19 Very Short Stories from My Life*, pp. 16-18.

[195] Source: Jett Wells, "The Most LEGENDARY College Pranks (PHOTOS)." Huffington Post. 3 June 2010. <http://www.huffingtonpost.com/2010/06/03/legendary-college-pranks_n_599731.html>.

[196] Source: Martin Sheridan, *Comics and Their Creators: Life Stories of American Cartoonists*, p. 110.

[197]Source: Gerald Nachman, *Seriously Funny*, p. 253.

[198]Source: James Fadiman and Robert Frager, *Essential Sufism*, p. 110.

[199]Source: S. Felix Mendelsohn, *Here's a Good One*, p. 249.

[200] Source: "Funny things said in prayers" thread. CougarUteForum.com. BYU/Utah/LDS Sports Forum and Message Board. <http://cougaruteforum.com/showthread.php?t=37014>. Accessed 26 December 2010.

[201] Source: Rabbi Dr. H. Rabinowicz, *A Guide to Hassidism*, p. 29.

[202] Source: Alyene Porter, *Papa was a Preacher*, p. 56.

[203] Source: Cal and Rose Samra, *Holy Hilarity*, pp. 69-70.

[204] Source: William H. Sessions, collector, *Laughter in Quaker Grey*, p. 71.

[205] Source: Neal Shusterman, *Kid Heroes: True Stories of Rescuers, Survivors, and Achievers*, pp. 35-36.

[206] Source: Eileen Birin, compiler and editor, *Chalkboard Dust*, pp. 210-217.

[207] Source: Frances Alda, *Men, Women, and Tenors*, pp. 61-62, 112-113.

[208] Source: Bill Smoot, *Conversations with Great Teachers*, p. 16.

[209] Source: Barbara Eisenberg, *Conversations with Frank Gehry*, pp. 30, 33.

[210] Source: Nigel Douglas, *More Legendary Voices*, pp. 109-110.

[211] Source: Dick King-Smith, *Chewing the Cud*, pp. 187-188.

[212] Source: Henry T. Finck, *Musical Laughs*, p. 107.

[213] Source: John Boyden, collector, *Stick to the Music: Scores of Orchestral Tales*, p. 48.

[214] Source: Helen White Charles, collector and editor, *Quaker Chuckles*, p. 93.

[215] Source: Evangelia Callas, *My Daughter Maria Callas*, p. 65.

[216] Source: Barry Hewlett-Davies, *A Night at the Opera*, pp. 82, 140.

[217] Source: Colonel J.H. Mapleson, *The Mapleson Memoirs*, p. 235.

[218] Source: Philip Goodman, *Rejoice in Thy Festival*, p. 19.

[219] Source: Louis Michaels, *The Humor and Warmth of Pope John XXIII*, pp. 16-17.

[220] Source: Leslie Ayre, *The Wit of Music*, p. 28.

[221] Source: Marjorie Lawrence, *Interrupted Melody: The Story of My Life*, p. 133.

[222] Source: Shmuel Himelstein, *A Touch of Wisdom, A Touch of Wit*, pp. 252-253.

[223] Source: Shmuel Himelstein, *Words of Wisdom, Words of Wit*, p. 65.

[224] Source: Colonel J.H. Mapleson, *The Mapleson Memoirs*, pp. 131-132.

[225] Source: William H. Sessions, collector, *More Quaker Laughter*, p. 65.

[226] Source: Helen L. Kaufmann, *Anecdotes of Music and Musicians*, pp. 184-185.

[227] Source: William H. Sessions, collector, *Laughter in Quaker Grey*, p. 69.

[228] Source: Peg Bracken, *A Window Over the Sink*, p. 16.

[229] Source: Victor Borge and Robert Sherman, *My Favorite Comedies in Music*, p. 80.

[230] Source: Mina Carson, Tisa Lewis, and Susan M. Shaw, *Girls Rock! Fifty Years of Women Making Music*, p. 74.

[231] Source: Yitta Halberstam Mandelbaum, *Holy Brother*, pp. 160-161.

[232] Source: Neville Cardus, editor, *Kathleen Ferrier: A Memoir*, pp. 98-99.

[233] Source: Bruce Nash and Allan Zullo, *The Greatest Sports Stories Never Told*, pp. 44-46.

[234] Source: Ted Rall, "How US Ignorance Helped Doom the Afghan War." Commondreams.org. 29 July 2010 <http://www.commondreams.org/view/2010/07/29-12>.

[235] Source: Irvin C. Poley and Ruth Verlenden Poley, *Friendly Anecdotes*, pp. 117-118.

[236] Source: Evangelia Callas, *My Daughter Maria Callas*, p. 48.

[237] Source: Ernest Goldstein, *The Journey of Diego Rivera*, p. 94.

[238] Source: Benjamin Hoff, *The Way to Life: At the Heart of the* Tao Te Ching, pp. 7, 62, 81-82.

[239] Source: Jack Kornfield and Christina Feldman, *Soul Food*, pp. 255-256.

[240] Source: Luke Chan, *101 Lessons of Tao*, pp. 103, 116.

[241] Source: Marjorie Lawrence, *Interrupted Melody: The Story of My Life*, pp. 91-92.

[242] Source: David L. Groover and Cecil C. Conner, Jr., *Skeletons from the Opera Closet*, p. 125.

[243] Source: Michael J. Rosen, editor, *Horse People: Writers and Artists on the Horses They Love*, pp. 131-133.

[244] Source: Jeffrey K. Salkin, *Being God's Partner*, p. 44.

[245] Source: Tanaquil Le Clercq, *The Ballet Cook Book*, pp. 324-325.

[246] Source: Jeffrey K. Salkin, *Being God's Partner*, p. 29.

[247] Source: Irvin C. Poley and Ruth Verlenden Poley, *Friendly Anecdotes*, p. 66.

[248]Source: Lucien Stryk and Takashi Ikemoto, selectors and translators, *Zen: Poems, Prayers, Sermons, Anecdotes, Interviews*, pp. xxxviii-xxxix.

[249]Source: Chih Chung Tsai, *Zen Speaks*, p. 24.

[250]Source: Sharon Salzberg, *A Heart as Wide as the World*, pp. 44-45.